Until now, no book has served the millions of fathers of aborted children.
Most have stuck their r
Aborted shows how the
It also shows the only v
Dr. Marvin Olask
and Liberty, and author

MW01089153

Abortion takes the life of more than the single innocent one in the womb. The lives of both the potential mother and father, lives that might have been, are wiped out as well. This book is for the second of those two givers of life, the father. The good news of this book is that there is still a Life Giver, who heals wounded souls and raises the dead to life.
Michael Card, musician and author of *A Violent Grace*

Fatherhood Aborted is a clarion call of hope to those who have directly or indirectly failed and suffered the sorrow of a decision to abort a child. Far more, it is a commanding look at what a father is meant to be to his children and to his world. I read this work with sorrow and joy. Guy Condon passed from this earth before his book was published, yet his powerful words and life call us to be guardians of relationship and prophets of reconciliation in an area of such shame and acrimony. Guy Condon is my hero and my hope of what I would like to become as a man and as a father. Condon and Hazard have struck a chord for life even for those who have lived under the shadow of death.
Dan B. Allender, Ph.D., president, Mars Hill Graduate School, Seattle, Washington, and author of *The Wounded Heart, Cry of the Soul,* and *The Healing Path*

Guy Condon's life was characterized by devotion to God and service to man. Notwithstanding his "untimely" death, Guy's legacy continues with the publication of this book. *Fatherhood Aborted* details the devastating and often overlooked impact that abortion has on men and offers the hope of healing that can come only when men reconnect with their heavenly Father. Guy was a blessing to all who knew him. He will continue to bless all who read this book.
Ken Connor, president, Family Research Council

We knew abortion destroyed babies and exploited women. But Guy Condon and David Hazard clearly and biblically demonstrate the toll it has taken on men. This is must reading for those who care about life.
Gary L. Bauer, president, American Values

This is an unusual book because it examines abortion from the perspective of the father. Honest. Probing. And long overdue.
Dr. Luder G. Whitlock Jr., president of Reformed Theological Seminary

In all my years of counseling and listening to men, I have never seen a more reflective, helpful, and honest book on helping empty-armed fathers confront their pain. Yet Guy and David's book takes us further. It shows us the hope that confused and struggling men can find as they experience God's healing forgiveness and grace!

Dr. Gary Rosberg, president of America's Family Coaches and coauthor, with Barbara Rosberg, of *5 Love Needs of Men and Women*

This is not "just another book on abortion." Have you ever read one predicated on the tragic experience of "aborted fathers"? Males involved in the abortion of their unborn child may expect to go through a more painful, mind-shocking, and remorseful aftermath than they ever imagined possible. The authors of this insightful and compelling book tell why. This is highly recommended reading for postabortive men and also for those who by means of judicious foresight can avoid the anguish and suffering delineated in this remarkable volume.

D. James Kennedy, Ph.D., senior minister, Coral Ridge Presbyterian Church, Fort Lauderdale, Florida

It's about time someone gave hope to the fathers who are broken by abortion. The wounds these men suffer do not just go away with time. They continue to resurface, and the long-term effects are just as crippling and devastating to men as they are to women. Here's a book full of healing and hope, of love and forgiveness.

Hunter Tylo, television/film actress and founder of Hunter's Chosen Child

Fatherhood Aborted digs deep beneath the surface to shine the light of truth on the havoc and devastation wrought in the lives of men—and there are millions of them—when they actively or passively participate in aborting the life of a child. It also shows them the way to freedom, healing, and wholeness. This book could help heal the soul of America!

Bill McCartney, founder and president, Promise Keepers

Guy's love for the Lord and his compassion for postabortive people was extremely rare. His book gives men and the women who love them the key to healing. *Fatherhood Aborted* will definitely be Guy's legacy.

Linda Cochrane, executive director of Hopeline Women's Center, Danbury, Connecticut, and author of *Forgiven and Set Free: A Post-Abortion Bible Study for Women*

What a powerful message of reconciliation and restoration for the millions of silent partners in abortion. Every personal testimony in this book contains a jewel of healing for these men (and women) to help them experience the fullness of forgiveness and the refreshing of the Lord.

Star Parker, president of C.U.R.E. (Coalition on Urban Renewal and Education) and author of *How the Poor Get Rich*

Fatherhood
Aborted

Fatherhood
Aborted

Guy Condon
and
David Hazard

Tyndale House Publishers, Inc.
Wheaton, Illinois

Visit Tyndale's exciting Web site at www.tyndale.com

Fatherhood Aborted

Designed by Timothy R. Botts with Luke Daab

Edited by Susan Taylor and Dan Benson

Library of Congress Cataloging-in-Publication Data

Condon, Guy, date.
    Fatherhood aborted / Guy Condon and David Hazard.
        p. cm.
    Includes bibliographical references.
    ISBN 0-8423-5423-9 (sc)
    1. Abortion—Psychological aspects. 2. Fathers—Psychology. 3. Men—Psychology.
4. Abortion—Religious aspects—Christianity. I. Hazard, David. II. Title.

HQ767.C59 2001
306.874'2—dc21   2001027220

ISBN 0-8423-5423-9

Printed in the United States of America

07   06   05   04   03   02   01
 7   6   5   4   3   2   1

To Linnie
and my girls

CONTENTS

ACKNOWLEDGMENTS

WARREN WILLIAMS is an extraordinary man. The insights in the book, as well as the path of healing from the devastation of abortion that you will read about in this book, I owe to him. For years, Warren has searched the Scriptures and learned to walk with Christ—and as a result, his counsel to postabortive men has a grace and power that have brought freedom and new life to many.

Much gratitude goes to the men who bare their souls in this book. Because of the sensitive nature of this material their names and the names of their spouses have been changed for the sake of privacy. But without their willingness to walk through the fire of change—and then to share the painful, powerful, wonderful changes inside—this book would lack the dramatic witness of Christ's redeeming power in the lives of real men.

On the Death of GUY CONDON, November 11, 2000

A STRONG MAN OF GOD is in the presence of God while we grieve his loss and miss his infectious smile and tender heart. An intense fighter for life has lost his life; rather, we have lost his life while he has found the new life he longed and lived for.

On November 11, Guy was out doing what he did so well and so often. He was speaking on behalf of the unborn and asking those who attended the annual dinner to support the Capitol Hill Crisis Pregnancy Center in Washington, D.C., one of the CareNet affiliates Guy led. Under his presidency and dynamic leadership the number of CareNet centers grew to more than six hundred across the United States and Canada.

Guy finished his talk and headed home with his seventeen-year-old daughter, Mae. That Mae was with him that night speaks volumes about the quality of fatherhood Guy demonstrated to his children. While many teenagers could care less what their parents think or say, Mae had gone to hear her father speak. Many teens won't spend an extra minute in the same room with their parents, but Mae was along for the ride so she could spend time with her father. Guy was a rare and dedicated dad.

Guy loved his four daughters dearly and missed them intensely when he was away. As their lives unfolded, he became more passionate about his fight for the lives of the unborn. The joy his children brought him motivated him to reach further and wider to protect the children that would not have the chance to become the wonderful people his daughters had become.

As Guy and Mae were traveling home, a drunk driver broadsided them. Mae suffered a mild concussion and was treated and

released, but Guy took a direct hit and died on the way to the
hospital.

No one will miss Guy more than his wife, Linda, known as
"Linnie" to those who knew her best. He met her in Belgium
while he was on a mission trip to work with young people. He
played the guitar for them and talked to them about Jesus, sharing what Jesus had done in his life. That is where Guy found
Linda and where Linda discovered Guy's heart for God and
for God's people. During a time when some Christian leaders
talked one way and lived another, Guy was faithfully consistent.
His commitment to Linda was unwavering and their marriage a
godly example. Guy admired Linda and respected her strengths
and God-given talents. She stood in the wings of his ministry,
encouraging him to live his dream of making abortion an
option that no woman had to take out of desperation.

With Linda's encouragement, Guy took up the cause of life
for the unborn in 1988 while serving as president of Americans
United for Life. Everyone wanted a political victory against
abortion, but Guy was also concerned about the proper course
until there could be a political victory—or if a political victory
never occurred. While he was an ardent supporter of a consti-
tutional amendment to outlaw the abortion of unborn children, until that passed, he encouraged others to do what they
could do to save as many yet-to-be born lives as possible. Now,
ten years later, his wisdom has become the predominant strat-
egy of the pro-life movement.

With Guy's passing, the pro-life voice will be less articulate
and forceful until God raises up another to speak as well and
work as hard as Guy Condon. The integrity of his heart and
the eloquence of his communication style moved countless
individuals to rethink abortion as an option of convenience.

For twenty years Guy had taken up the fight that was considered a "women's issue." He courageously waded in as a man
who cared about women and understood the pain of those
struggling with a crisis pregnancy. In 1993 he left Americans
United for Life and took the helm of CareNet. There he not
only labored to save the lives of the unborn, but he expanded

the focus of the CareNet centers to include the pregnant and confused mothers. He motivated all of us to "love them both." His compassion for the mothers gave them an identity beyond the label of "murderer," a label that the less caring had assigned them through verbal abuse and written word. While many only yelled and screamed at those who supported a woman's right to an abortion, Guy used his voice to raise millions of dollars to protect the unborn from premature death.

As president of CareNet, Guy led the nation's largest Christian outreach to pregnant women who were in crisis or unaware of alternatives to abortion. CareNet centers offer women free pregnancy tests, pregnancy counseling, medical and adoption referrals, parenting and birthing classes, maternity and baby clothes, baby food and furniture, and even training on how to manage a family budget or hold down a paying job. Under Guy's leadership this dynamic organization grew to include 1,000 paid staff, 20,000 volunteers, and 300,000 local supporters involved in caring for 290,000 women with unplanned pregnancies in communities all across America and Canada. Of those women, 90 percent decided to bring their pregnancies to full term, many of them accepting Christ in the process.

Perhaps the most noteworthy of all Guy's projects was the National Campaign of Compassion, which has helped thousands of women discover that there is an alternative to abortion. In 1998, Guy announced that CareNet would place five thousand billboards in strategic locations, offering help to women experiencing an unwanted pregnancy. Through this program Guy advertised a central phone number that allowed women to talk directly to the pregnancy center nearest them. The campaign was a phenomenal success, and by the year 2000 arrangements were in place for eight thousand billboards to carry the message of hope. The billboards were so simple that within seconds a person traveling down a major freeway could take in the message. The one word caption, "Pregnant?" captured readers' attention and offered 800-395-HELP as a

xvi

resource for confidential help. It was and is the largest public-service campaign in the history of outdoor advertising.

The numbers testify to the success of the program: In 1999, the centers processed more than 43,000 phone calls for help. By the end of 1999 they were logging in excess of 5,000 calls a month, more than 150 in an average day. Some CareNet centers have reported a 50 percent increase in the number of phone calls they received after billboards went up in their area.

GETTING PERSONAL

Upon Guy's death, the *Washington Times* quoted CareNet board chairman, Susan Olasky: "Guy was a bridge builder with a rare combination of intellect and compassion. His tireless commitment to all those affected by abortion was inspiring to all of us." The "all" that Guy was committed to helping included the men who had either walked away or had pressured someone to have an abortion. He built a bridge to those men who had no place to hide and no place to heal from the shame of allowing their own children to be killed.

I was one of those men. When faced with a pregnant girlfriend, I pressured her to abort our child. When this wonderful young woman and our baby needed me to be a man, I was anything but a man. I sacrificed my own baby for the sake of my image, my convenience, and my destructive ego. With no one to turn to, either before or after the abortion, I wallowed alone in my sickness and shame. Ulcers threatened my life as the effects of guilt came to bear on me. I had made a move in haste, just to get it all out of the way, but it has never moved out of the way. I think of that decision almost everyday.

Years after the abortion, my wife and I discovered we were an infertile couple. I had once been able to create life and had destroyed it; now I would never be able to create life again. But God had a great plan of restoration for my wife and me. On December 24, 1990, our daughter, Madeline, was born to her sixteen-year-old birth parents. Faced with the same crisis I had encountered years earlier, they had the courage I did not have.

They made a decision for life and a decision for parenthood for my wife and me. We will forever be indebted to them for allowing us to be parents and to raise this most remarkable child. She is the joy of our lives and proof that only God can take the source of your greatest pain and transform it into the source of your greatest joy.

Guy knew my story and how abortion and adoption had changed my life. He invited me to share my experiences with the leaders of CareNet centers all across America. I remember the Fort Worth conference where I spoke and met so many dedicated women running those centers. Guy was there, encouraging the staff and solving problems for those he served. I don't think he ever took off the cowboy hat they lovingly presented to their leader and hero.

The year before his death, Guy worked diligently on this book project to more effectively educate men about abortion and to reach out to those suffering in the aftermath. His desire was to see men whose hearts had been broken find healing from the pain of their tragic decision to abandon and destroy the children they helped to create. I am grateful that God allowed Guy to finish this project because it has provided a new dimension of healing for me.

This book pierces our culture's deafening silence about the aftereffects of abortion. Guy writes, "For most of us, keeping important matters to ourselves is, purely and simply, a basic survival skill." But then he asks, "Can't we talk about abortion and its long-lasting effect on a man's life?" Guy's final accomplishment shows us that our way out of mere survival and into fulfillment and purpose is to break the silence, to face reality, and to talk about our past and our pain. Guy does not whisper through this book. Instead, he cries out to men to find a better way to live, free from the condemnation and shame abortion brings to men. Any man tired of running from his past can stop here and find rest in God's grace.

None of us will ever know how profound Guy's impact has been on this modern culture of convenience and death. He was not perfect; I just never saw any of his imperfections. I want to be more like him. I want God to give me his humility and his servant heart. I want Guy's lack of pretense and his ability to change the hearts of men and women who have given up hope. I am so glad he took the time and expended the effort to share his heart through this book. It is a guide for all of us men who need healing. It is also a path toward the godly manhood we broken men are searching to find.

It is my prayer that in reading this book you will discover Guy's heart and the heart of God. And that Guy's words will help you discover God's extravagant grace and boundless love that will inspire you to live beyond the frivolous standard of manhood our society requires. There is truth here. Search diligently for it so that you might find the freedom that our Lord and Savior desires for you.

Stephen Arterburn
January 2001

FOREWORD

GUY CONDON AND DAVID HAZARD may qualify as the proverbial
fools who dare to tread where angels fear to go, but what they've
written here is gutsy stuff. With over 40 million abortions performed in America since 1973, there are millions of "walking
wounded" out there, silently suffering from its debilitating
aftereffects. And they're not just women. They're men, and
they're all around us. They're our fathers, grandfathers, uncles,
brothers, nephews, sons, and friends—men who have participated either willingly or unwillingly in the death of an unborn
child. Indeed, "they" just might be "us."

Fatherhood Aborted is a truly courageous book. As the authors
mention, it's okay for men to discuss almost anything. They
are encouraged to reveal the most intimate details of their lives
on afternoon talk shows, delving shamelessly into subjects that
should make us blush—but the effects of abortion remain one
of the few "taboo" issues of our day.

But whether our society acknowledges it or not, involvement
in the abortion of his child leaves a deep wound in a man's
soul, a wound that can cripple him in many areas of his life,
but particularly in his relationships and *especially* as a father. Like
some ugly sea monster, an abortion in a man's past lurks rest-
lessly in the dark recesses of his soul, leaving a trail of guilt and
shame that stains everything he does and that can prevent him
from achieving true manhood.

The good news is that there is hope and help for postabortive
men. No sin is beyond the cleansing power of the blood of
Christ. Guy Condon and David Hazard not only do a wonderful job of exposing the devastating effects abortion has on men,

they go on to point men to the path of healing and restoration—to forgivenss, to manhood redeemed, and fatherhood restored. If there is an abortion in your past, it's likely that among other things, you have trouble with commitment, with authority, with bonding with your wife or children. You may also have irrational fears about losing those you love. You *need* to read this book.

Sadly, coauthor Guy Condon died in a tragic car accident before this book was published. But *Fatherhood Aborted* serves as a glorious capstone to his life—a life dedicated to helping men and women avoid the awful "choice" of abortion, to ministering to those who suffer from the devastating aftereffects of that decision, and to saving unborn babies from death. Guy may be gone, but he has left a wonderful legacy of heroic service to our almighty God, of laboring in a difficult field of hardened earth and buried stones. Some of the fruit of Guy's labor is here. I pray the Lord will use it to bring healing to millions of men in America, to renew a spirit of genuine fatherhood in our land, and perhaps even to help restore the crippled soul of our nation.

Bill McCartney
Founder and president,
Promise Keepers

Memorial Introduction:
Sometimes Plans Change

If things had gone according to our plan, you would have been reading an introduction by Guy Condon, and I would have remained all but invisible to you. That's often been the case with the books I've cowritten. I'm a private guy.

True, I've been involved in pro-life work for many years, serving on the board of a national ministry, helping my wife and others to found a local crisis pregnancy center, even counseling postabortive women and men. But Guy, my friend and cowriter, was to be the front man for this book. Like me, Guy was passionate about helping men recover from the spiritual and emotional damage that inevitably come in the aftershocks of abortion. Since he was president of CareNet, a pro-life organization with some eight hundred affiliate members, and a well-loved speaker in the pro-life movement, the plan for him to step forward as the "lead voice" in this case made most sense.

But things did not go according to our plan.

On a Sunday morning, early, the phone call came—with news I didn't want to believe.

I drove quickly to Guy's home, just a mile from mine, white-knuckling the steering wheel. Our youngest daughters are best friends. I prayed, *Don't let this be true.*

When Lin greeted me at the door, her face told me this was no misshapen rumor. Guy had been driving to his home in rural Virginia after speaking at a fund-raising dinner for a crisis pregnancy center in Washington, D.C. Crossing one of the worst intersections in our county, he was struck broadside by an oncoming van. One of his daughters, who'd been with him, was home resting, having suffered a moderate concussion.

Guy was gone.

There is not much you can do at a time like that to ease, or even touch, the awful hurt. Lin and I hugged; we cried. There is not much that you can say to describe the empty gap that's left inside when a husband . . . or friend . . . is suddenly gone.

Days later, my family and I were among hundreds who packed St. Peter's Episcopal Church in Purcellville, Virginia, for Guy's memorial service. The strained faces—of family members, of local friends, of national leaders in the pro-life movement—showed we all felt, in various measures, that same awful gap.

When Guy's spiritual director gave the message, I began to sense the real enormity of the hole left by Guy's untimely passing. He spoke of Guy's passion. I'd seen that fire up close. Guy was passionate about wanting to save the lives of unborn children, tireless in his work to help spare women not only the pain of loss, but also the physical and spiritual damage of abortion. I'd also felt in him a pulse that was urgent about helping men, the often misunderstood and ignored victims of the abortion industry.

As the speaker continued, I could almost hear Guy saying, "Men are not the terrible *perpetrators* of a crime against women and unborn babies, the way they've often been portrayed. Men are wounded in their spirits and emotions, and their lives become painfully limited from any kind of involvement with abortion. They don't need more judgment. They need to know how to become whole men again."

It was at about this point that the speaker reminded us of a statement Jesus made in reference to his own death: "Unless a grain of wheat falls into the earth and dies, it remains alone; but if it dies, it bears much fruit" (John 12:24, RSV). In the economy of God, the speaker reminded us, new life and great things can always come forth from death . . . if we have the eyes to see God's purposes . . . and the courage to act on what we see. He was convinced some of us would see the passion in Guy's life, perhaps more now in his absence and that the passions in his heart would now fill us as well.

"And so I ask you," the speaker said in closing, "what will you do with Guy's heart?"

He was not looking directly at me, but he might as well have been.

In the quiet moment that followed, a picture came to my mind's eye. I saw my good friend, Guy Condon. He'd been out on the front lines of an enormous struggle, not just to stop abortion but also to help and heal those whose choice to end another life has deeply hurt every part of their own lives. It was like watching a war buddy charging courageously into battle, carrying a standard. The standard read *Mercy for All.* And then I saw Guy falling, the standard dropping from his hand. . . .

Sometimes plans change. Yes, you can remain behind the scenes. Let others wage the fight. Or you can step up, reach out, and before the standard hits the ground, catch it in your own hand. You can take up where another has fallen and trust in the mysteries of providence that even more good will come of this.

I cannot begin to fill the gap left by my friend's passing. But I will be taking a more active role with men, especially, who need to experience forgiveness and healing in the aftermath of abortion.

But this book is, and always will be, to me, Guy's standard. It honors him and all the energies of life he gave to heal the suffering of others. Tyndale House and I, together, offer it to you. We know that the healing steps it offers will lead you or someone you know to a spiritual and emotional wholeness in place of the wounds left in the wake of abortion.

I can tell you one thing for sure: Even if you've believed the game plan for your life was set . . . maybe even hopelessly, unchangeably marred by your past . . .

Sometimes plans change.

David Hazard
January 2001

Introduction:
The Secret Men Need
to Talk About

It's midday. A TV talk show features three men discussing their former cocaine addictions with a recovery counselor. It's gritty stuff—one guy had even forced his wife into prostitution to support his habit. On a radio program a man describes his compulsive gambling and how he sold his little girl's bedroom furniture and bike to pay debts. Later, on one of those television "magazine" shows, a university administrator goes public to admit that he's a sexual predator who harasses female students. He can't help himself.

To a man, they talk about the stress or pain that drove them to their bad choices. The on-air hosts, the guest counselors, and the audiences applaud their bravery for admitting they have a problem.

Today, it's okay for a man to admit to struggles and pain—and even wrongdoing—for almost every problem under the sun. Almost.

There's one problem many men bear alone. I'm referring to the damage that spreads through a man's life when he is involved in the act of abortion. It doesn't matter whether he forcefully argued with his girlfriend to "get rid of it" or got the wind knocked out of his gut by a phone call from her saying, "Sorry, it's a done deal." When a man has fathered a child and that child's life is terminated by the unnatural and violent act of abortion, a destructive chain reaction silently begins in his life.

As president of a national pro-life organization that supports crisis pregnancy centers and clinics around the United States, I've met hundreds of men suffering from the impact of abortion, and they come from all walks of life. Abortive fathers may be young single men of high school or college age. But they may also be married men whose wives had an abortion. They are educated and uneducated; they may be wealthy or have average or low incomes. They may be faithful churchgoers or those who profess no faith. They may have been willing participants in the abortion, perhaps urging the women to have the abortion and even paying for it. Or they may have been unwilling participants who had little or no say in the decision to abort the child. They may be fathers of one or several aborted children.

I've also worked with counselors who know thousands more of these men than I do. The pain and remorse these men carry is staggering. Abortion can have a negative effect on every part of a man's life—his emotions, his soul, his relationships, his work and career, and most definitely his relationship with God.

What makes the problem worse is silence. Why, when men and society are now dealing openly with every other issue, can't men talk about abortion and its long-lasting damage to a man's life?

There is help and healing to be found, but it begins with breaking the silence.

Consider just a few of the forces that leave a man struggling on his own.

WALLS OF SILENCE

First, there is a deafening silence in our culture about the terrible aftershocks of abortion itself. Certain forces in our society have successfully sold the line that abortion is a "choice" a woman makes, on par with any other. They admit that it's a serious choice, but only because the decision about whether to have a baby affects a woman's physical body and lifestyle. According to their argument, a woman's choice in this area has no greater moral or emotional significance than her choice of which cola drink she likes best. A woman must be completely free to choose.

Ironically—maybe hypocritically—these same forces get very uncomfortable when a woman later wants to exercise her right of free speech and talk openly about the devastating consequences of terminating the life that was growing in her womb. Why don't we see TV talk shows featuring the many women who have suffered physically, emotionally, and spiritually after having an abortion? Because we're supposed to think that the problem was merely an unplanned or unwanted pregnancy. We're not supposed to question a "medical procedure" that ends life, leaves physical damage, breaks up couples, and scars the soul.

> **There is a deafening silence in our culture about the terrible aftershocks of abortion.**

The sad truth is that many churches and individual Christians help keep this cultural silence in place. They're uncomfortable talking about abortion, sometimes because they don't want to offend anyone or because they think it's better to keep their children from hearing about the harsh realities of life.

The truth is this: Right now our culture does not welcome open discussion about the effects of abortion on anyone, male or female. In a so-called open society this is a travesty. In the spiritual community we must continue our move toward open help and support.

"SAFETY" IN SILENCE

The second reason we haven't talked about the effects of abortion on men is that men know silence can be a safe zone. We learn early in our lives that simply not talking can be our fortress—our cave. At school we offer a wrong answer . . . and get laughed at. Later our girlfriends or wives press us for answers . . . and we soon figure out that treating them to stony silence makes them end the siege and go away. We'll do almost anything to avoid being mocked, pressured, or made to feel "small." In silence we think that nothing and no one can get to us or squash us. If we're quiet long enough, the "enemy" will just go away.

This tactic comes naturally, I think, from our typically private nature as men. Intimacy and personal openness are not usually locations on the male "emotional map." When did it ever appear manly to talk about very private matters or about what's going on inside us? No man—not your coach, your shop teacher, your flight commander, or your boss—ever sat you down and asked, "How do you feel?" Because they were men, they all respected your natural desire for privacy. So leave the emotional probing and tears to Oprah Winfrey.

Here's the bottom line: For most men, keeping important matters to ourselves is, purely and simply, a basic survival skill. Our hopes, our opinions, and we hope, our secrets all survive intact because we've learned to shut up.

Few things feel more personal and private than having had an intimate relationship, helping to conceive a child, and then seeing its life ended. And few things have greater impact on a man's life, hitting him with the emotional force of an asteroid slamming the earth.

The net effect is this: There is little in our natural makeup as men that prepares us to do the one thing we need to do: to talk openly and to honestly face the truth about the great damage to our souls when we, givers and protectors of life, abandon our instinctive responsibility for other lives.*

FACING THE TRUTH

The third reason we don't talk much about the impact of abortion on men is the very nature of abortion. But silence cannot hide this fact: When a doctor injects saline into a woman's womb or uses a powerful suction hose or metal instruments to extract the life growing in her, the doctor is burning or dismembering another human being—a baby.

This is brutal, I know, and not pleasant to read. But it's the truth. And starting over again, with the truth, is what puts every man on the road to wholeness, health, and full, real man-

---

*Note: Neither author is postabortive, but because of their strong identification with the struggles of men who are, they chose to use the pronouns *we* and *our* throught much of this book.

hood. We must be equipped to know the truth; otherwise, why would Jesus Christ have said that the truth will make us free?

Though self-protective silence is a skill we men learned early—and learned well—it isn't the only skill we need. Chris wouldn't tell anyone about the fatigue that had nagged him for months—until the leukemia had progressed too far to respond to treatment. Mike thought he should ignore his wife's pleas to get marriage counseling. ("Maybe she'll quit focusing on all these stupid little problems.") Then he came home to a set of divorce papers. There comes a time when a man has to learn to open up and talk, to find someone to help him face things he can't handle on his own. If not, his silence can be his undoing.

As men, many of us have thought that facing the truth would hurt us. Raising a wall of silence can keep other people from knowing things about us we wish we didn't know about ourselves. But our silence also gives power to the shame and the confusion that dog us wherever we go. We find ourselves feeling strangely isolated—not the confident, settled, focused men we want to be.

There is little in our natural makeup as men that prepares us to do the one thing we need to do: to honestly face the truth about the great damage to our souls when we, givers and protectors of life, abandon our instinctive responsibility for other lives.

Today many women are finding healing from the damage caused by their choice to abort a child. They know, all too painfully, that our past actions do affect us now. Likewise, every man who suffers silently from taking part in an abortion, whether willingly or unwillingly, can also find this wholeness and maturity.

I've prepared this book for just that purpose: to help courageous men who want to stop dodging and running from the sins and failures of the past. It is for every man who wants to stop allowing the past to dictate who he is right now.

YOU CAN BEGIN AGAIN

Abortion is a terrible crime against humankind. Most of all, it's a crime against the innocent unborn. But abortion also damages women and men, bringing its own set of destructive consequences to their lives.

As with every other sin, there is a way to find forgiveness, healing, and restoration—if we're brave enough to square our shoulders and take the right steps, beginning today.

If you're the father of an aborted child, following the steps in this book will be among the most challenging experiences you'll ever have. But it will also be one of the most rewarding. The stories you are about to read of other men who have been where you are, and the steps you're going to follow to forgiveness and wholeness, can change your life.

I can assure you of one thing: The decision to proceed is one you'll never regret.

One

The Fugitive

Ben has been driven by a hidden force for years.

Not "driven" in the sense that he's a maniac workaholic. Rather, he's vaguely aware that he runs from certain situations, avoids particular people. He'd like to see himself as a man who can face his problems, act with confidence—but the truth is, he sometimes knows he's running from challenges and a lot of things that make him uncomfortable. It doesn't make him feel good about himself.

Dimly, Ben is aware that in some ways he's like a fugitive, running from a truth he doesn't want to face. And he knows it began years ago with an event he'd like to erase.

In junior college he dated a woman, and within six months she was pregnant. They agreed that abortion was the best solution. He drove her to the clinic and nervously thumbed through magazines, waiting. He was not prepared for the dull pain he saw in her eyes when it was over.

Ben dropped her off at the sorority house, where a girlfriend would take care of her as she recovered. He walked out the door and kept going. He knew it was over.

They saw each other twice after that but never dated again. Ben wasn't particularly proud of himself, but hey, abortion happened to a lot of couples. Nobody had to know. That was the end of it.

But it was far from over. In a way, it had only begun.

PURSUED

Ben had mistakenly assumed that the calendar pages would flip and that he and his former girlfriend would simply go on to other lives. Time would cover their tracks.

He had no way of knowing that this one moment in time held an incredible, hidden power to pursue him.

Ben married eight years later and began a career in fiber-optic technology. Then one evening he came home to find that his wife had a candlelit dinner on the table—and special news. "I'm pregnant," she whispered, kissing his neck. "You're going to be a daddy."

A week later Ben awoke in a cold sweat, overwhelmed by an anxiety that left him twisting and turning in the dark. Fatherhood. Wasn't he supposed to be happy? Shouldn't he feel exhilarated about this "passage to manhood"?

In the cold light of dawn, as Ben dragged the razor over his face, he knew these were not the real questions. Somewhere inside, an accusing voice was asking, *What gives you the right to be a father now, when you once aborted a child? How will you be able to raise this child to be a decent person—to be loving, honest, or responsible—when you've failed at these things yourself?*

Months later their sweet little girl arrived, and Ben held her in his arms, admiring her perfect face, loving her on first sight. But the tears in his eyes were not entirely tears of joy.

He felt like such a hypocrite when his father clapped him on the shoulder and said, "Congratulations, Son." Why did the past have to wreck this moment?

MALE POSTABORTION TRAUMA

Promoters of abortion and the abortion industry would like us all to think that abortion is simple, safe, and easy, that terminating the life of a child in the womb is akin to avoiding pregnancy. In fact, its impact on the soul of both women and men is powerful and lasting.

Emotional confusion—like Ben's self-doubt, anxiety, and guilt at what should have been a joyous moment—is only one symptom that recurs in the life of any man who has experienced the abortion of his child. It can appear at seemingly inappropriate moments, such as the birth of another child, leaving confusion, remorse, guilt, depression. Some men like to deny that the past has any power over the present, but evidence clearly proves otherwise. What remains hidden and unresolved about the past does take on a life of its own, pursues us, and has the power to steal life from the present.

There is a range of other symptoms, or characteristics, that appear in the lives of men who have participated in abortion. Some are subtle, some life-dominating. These characteristics have led counselors and other professionals to recognize the reality of postabortion trauma in men, a force that can be every bit as real as the symptoms experienced by men who have witnessed atrocities in battle. Their symptoms have the power to rob men of full, peaceful, purposeful lives.

What are these other characteristics? If you are a man with abortion in your past, you may recognize some of the following forces at work within you. Not every post-abortive man will experience all of these symptoms, but it's likely that you will find more than one of them present in your life.

You Have Difficulty with Commitment

True, you recognize what's important and what deserves commitment. God. Church. Family. Job. Friends. Neighbors. But commitment means someone is going to count on you if you step forward and offer yourself, and this makes you uncomfortable. You learn to let other people carry the weight.

Or you may become enthusiastic and make a commitment, only to get cold feet and pull back. Soon this leaves people wondering what planet you're from and leaves you feeling embarrassed and foolish. That's when you stop getting involved and leave leadership to other guys.

The abortion industry would like us all to think that abortion is simple, safe, and easy, that terminating the life of a child in the womb is akin to avoiding pregnancy. In fact, its impact on the soul of both women and men is powerful and lasting.

Today, many men seem to have a problem living up to commitments. But the inability to take on and follow through with responsibility is epidemic among postabortive men. As a result, you become a somewhat detached, passive "bench sitter" in life.

Aftershocks of Male Postabortion Trauma

You have difficulty with commitment.
You dodge authority.
You have no solid sense of identity.
You work to impress moral leaders.
You keep women at bay.
You have trouble bonding.
You fear impending tragedy.
You don't own your mistakes.
You feel inadequate as a leader.

You Dodge Authority

You may really want a good relationship with the man or woman in charge. But when it comes down to it, bosses are there to make sure a job gets done and done well, and you don't like someone pushing you to reach higher standards. You may tell yourself that work is a pain because the boss is incompetent or unreasonable, but deep inside you know that the truth is much closer to home.

The truth? Many postabortive men hate being held accountable to someone else's standard. They seem to hold special contempt for anyone who might contradict or correct them.

This can cause serious problems on the job—or for that matter, in any setting where someone acts as an authority. These problems include being overreactive, biting and sarcastic; finding it difficult to be a team player; and having a tendency to get sulky when criticized.

You Have No Solid Sense of Identity

Long after other men have settled into their identity, you may
still experience a deep unsettledness in your personality or in
your life's direction.

A lot of adult men, even at midlife, are still saying, "I wish I
knew what I'm going to be when I grow up." But the unsettled
feeling you have goes deeper than that. Sometimes you feel like
a chameleon, shifting identities to suit the crowd you're with.
You dream about unrealized possibilities. ("Maybe I can quit
this lousy sales job and still get into medical school.") Or you
rationalize present sad realities and disappointments, often
blaming others. ("I could have gotten the breaks if I'd kissed
up to the right people. But I refuse to do that.")

Underneath it all, you sometimes feel like an unsure
adolescent. *Wasn't this unsteady path supposed to end with manhood?*
you wonder. *When did I reach manhood anyway?*

You Work to Impress Moral Leaders

In some ways this is the flip side of hating to be criticized by a
boss. You may despise having to live up to a standard, but you
really need someone to see the best in you. And after all, if the
most moral person you know—a godly man or woman—thinks
you're a great guy, isn't that a stamp of approval?

As with any serious sin, men who have taken part in abortion
can feel that they've been branded as moral failures—almost as
lesser forms of life. This can lead you into a host of religious
hypocrisies such as legalism or spouting party lines—not because
you believe those lines but because you're "supposed" to. Feeling like moral failures creates religious workaholics. It can drive
you to a false humility so that, whenever a moral leader compli-
ments you, you insist you're dogs and verbally roll over in the
dirt and degrade yourself.

If this symptom applies to you, the confusion that plagues
your emotions also shows up in your spiritual life. What matters
to you is that the spiritual leader thinks you're one of the most
upright, decent guys he knows. But a neon sign begins to flash
in your soul, shouting, *You don't deserve any praise.* As a result, when

someone recognizes the good work you do today, you respond
out of the unresolved wrong of your past.

You Keep Women at Bay

While authority figures and godly men raise certain issues in
your life, women who are decent, smart, and capable often
raise another: Many postabortive men harbor a deep-down
conviction that they don't deserve the company of a "good"
woman. As a result, they instinctively keep their distance
from women who have it together.

Some guys gravitate to women who are more needy. If a
postabortive man marries a more healthy, stable, capable
woman, he may maintain an emotional barrier to keep her
out of certain rooms in his soul. It's almost a religious commitment for him to protect this secret! Obviously, this can
lead to severe problems in the marriage.

You Have Trouble Bonding

Bonding, which most men joke about, is simply the healthy
ability to feel united and at peace with another person. We
all need bonds of trust, affection, honesty, and shared values.
We need other people to understand how we think and feel—
and we need to understand *them*—in order to be growing as
a whole person.

But for the postabortive man, bonding is often a problem.

Long after the abortion of a child, you may continue to
move from one loosely built relationship to another. You
tend to leave an invisible back door open "in case it doesn't
work out"—which ensures that it won't. If the woman you're
dating has children, you insist you love her but hadn't bar-
gained for a package that includes her kids.

Or you may be among the postabortive men who go on
to marry. Yet, even with a wedding ring on your finger, a deep
sense of detachment plagues your family relationships. There
are huge gulfs between you and your wife and between you and
your living children—gulfs created by secrets kept hidden, by
guilt unresolved. Open, honest conversation is rare.

You may give off confusing signals—sometimes letting others feel that you want them close, then suddenly growing cool in a way that tells them to back off. This leaves you distant and ineffective in the lives of people you truly love.

You Fear Impending Tragedy

Regardless of whether you're versed in classical myths, the story of Damocles may sound familiar to you.

Damocles was invited by a Greek king to a grand feast. Once comfortably seated, he looked up to see a sword dangling over him, held only by a weak thread. In days past, Damocles had criticized the king and boasted that he could do a better job. Now the king wanted to teach his guest a lesson: Damocles would feel what it was like to have life-and-death decisions hanging over his head. While everyone else was able to kick back and have a great time, Damocles had a rather nerve-racking evening—and he got the humbling message.

Like Damocles, many men who carry the shame and guilt of abortion live under the nagging fear that something terrible is about to fall upon them. Judgment day, in one form or another, is near. This sense of doom can lessen somewhat if they've had a spiritual awakening and asked God's forgiveness. And yet they suspect that, one day soon, their wife will get cancer or their health will fail or their career will take a nosedive.

The postabortive man may experience a special fear for the children he now has—fear that a child will be taken by accidental death or terminal illness. It's as if he believes God is waiting for him to form a deep, loving attachment just to suddenly snatch the child away and inflict maximum pain. If the man's wife should have a miscarriage, he may feel that God is getting even with him for aborting a child in the past.

As a result, postabortive men tend to live in a constant, subliminal state of anxiety. For some this leads to chronic, mild depression. A praying man's prayers may involve a lot of bargaining with God. He may believe God will let him into heaven,

but he's certain God will deliver a big, punishing blow before
then.

You Don't Own Your Mistakes

Okay, none of us like to be caught in a fault. Who does? But a
healthy, maturing man gives in once in a while. He accepts that
life has a big learning curve. He owns up to his failures—even
moral ones.

But a man who's failed to deal with the sin and tragedy of
abortion continues to labor through life beneath a load of
guilt. We all have a deeply embedded hope to be part of God's
wonderful plan to create new life, but as a participant in abortion, you know you went against the most fundamental laws of
living.

When you're carrying that much guilt, you wonder how you
could handle any more? So you've become a master at finding
ways to off-load your faults on everyone else. It's not that you
failed to get the project done on deadline—the client wanted
too much. If your girlfriend or wife doesn't like to argue, she
should accept you the way you are and leave you alone. If your
boss evaluates you critically, it's because he's a clown who
doesn't understand you or the job. If your kids don't like your
explosions, they should behave. And what does God know about
how tough it is to be a decent man? He lives surrounded by
angels; you live in New Jersey.

All the while, your life is marked by struggle, unhappiness,
lack of fulfillment. By blaming other people, you've given up
the inner peace and power that result from taking personal
responsibility.

You Feel Inadequate as a Leader

Every man is a leader. A few have the whole set of abilities it
takes to be leaders of masses. The rest of us are meant to lead
smaller "flocks"—and if nothing else, to exercise personal leadership. We can gain enough skill, at least, to provide vision,
support, and an example to our friends or family . . . and to
make a meaningful contribution with our lives.

But all leadership rests on authority—and authority comes when you're able to do what you're asking of others. When you participated in the killing of an unborn child, you let into your soul the voice that continually whispers, *You have no right to tell others that what they're doing is wrong.* And when you have to speak against moral wrongs—whether to a child or an embezzler—you struggle against an adversary within. And most often, you lose.

As a postabortive man, you may experience a sense of powerlessness over evil and wrongdoing. An unclear conscience closes the door to vision and interrupts your ability to complete the tasks that are before you. You may imagine that you can never gain a place of moral leadership again, because to stand for what's good and right now would only make you a hypocrite.

Can you ever be free from those inner accusations that come when you want to direct your children in what's right and wrong? when you want to give leadership to other men? or stand for morality in a public setting?

THE GREAT IRONY

Some of these symptoms or characteristics may leap off the page at you because, to some degree, you see them at work in your life today. Others may seem foreign. As I said before, abortion may have been forced on you by a woman who was unwilling to carry your child. Yet there is one thing that seems to link together all men who face the long-term effects of abortion: a horrific sense of loss.

Deep within the soul of every man who's been involved in abortion, a truth repeats itself: *The life of my child, the fruit of my own body, has been lost.* And that is not the only thing. In the aftershocks of this terrible event, a man soon comes to realize: *The life I could have had—the husband, the father, the man I could have been—is lost.*

There is one thing that seems to link together all men who face the long-term effects of abortion: a horrific sense of loss.

And so we come to the great irony of abortion.

Adults most often commit the act of abortion to "save" themselves from responsibilities they do not want or to "spare" themselves from living with the knowledge that their child is "out there somewhere." But when you sacrifice a life to save yourself, you are struck with the force of interior aftershocks—like those we've just explored—and you cannot escape or ignore them.

The man who believed that one visit to a clinic ended the problem instead finds himself a fugitive, pursued by events of the past.

Is this your predicament?

Can you ever be the man you'd like to be—reconciled with yourself and with God? At peace? A man capable of having healthy relationships with the women and children in your life? Can you stop being defined by some force from the past?

Yes, you can.

TURNING IT AROUND

It dawned on Sam, when some guys from the neighborhood took him to some dirt-bike races, that being alive means being happy and at peace. These guys were fun, full of life. He'd been fighting mild depression, merely existing. Sam wanted to feel free to embrace life but couldn't. When he finally faced the grief he'd been pushing away for four years—grief for the child he'd abandoned through abortion—he began to feel alive again.

Rick was watching his marriage and family fall apart. "I love you," Carol told him, "but the kids and I need to separate from you until you can stop being so rigid. To you, being a Christian is all laws and rule keeping. We can't handle your making us feel guilty anymore." When Rick admitted that his family was paying for his own moral failures—which, in college, had led to two abortions—he finally sought the help that allowed him to experience forgiveness. And new, trusting, maturing relationships began to grow in his family.

Terry hit a brick wall the morning his fourteen-year-old daughter squared off with him and contended, "What's the big deal about abortion? Shouldn't a woman have the right to choose what's best for her and her own body? And what if a couple just doesn't want to have a kid?" He'd opened his mouth, but nothing came out . . . because a voice inside was shouting, *Don't be a hypocrite!* When Terry confessed his sin to a counselor, he began to see how much moral leadership he'd given up in his daughter's life—and began to see how he could regain his rightful role.

Sam, Rick, Terry—these are just a few of the men who are overcoming the far-reaching effects abortion has in a man's life. You can overcome those effects too and experience true peace and victory in your life.

Maybe you've thought the past is a place you just don't want to revisit. What good would it do? How can mucking around in the past change anything? But such thinking denies the truth that the past has a powerful effect on the present. Only by facing up to your past can you overcome its devastating consequences. And only then can you begin the healing process that leads to liberation.

This book will help you begin to recognize the deep impact of abortion on your life. It draws on the experiences of men who have dealt with abortion's devastation, as well as the wisdom of counselors who have helped them. As you read, you'll gain:

I. A clear picture of inner forces that may be driving you. Maybe you've already seen something of yourself in the men you've read about or in the characteristics described above. The truth is, every one of us needs help to escape old tendencies and find strength to grow.

2. Healing from wounds of the past. As men, we don't like to see ourselves as wounded—because that creates a picture of a poor, weak, bruised, limping person. Not exactly the virile, in-charge image we like to have of ourselves. But guilt and shame are wounds to the inner man, so are grief, remorse, sorrow, and depression.

In one way, men have been given a gift. Most of us have

the ability to ignore pain, and this serves us well in war, sports, and the working world. But ignoring pain doesn't work in every sphere of life. Ignoring pain in our relationships doesn't make us men. It makes us guys who don't know how to deal with life's wide range of realities—which includes all kinds of hard and messy things. It keeps us from living life to the full, in the present. In some cases, the best we've been able to say to our wives, our children, or ourselves is, "So it hurts. So what? Don't think about it." An inability to face up to pain betrays our lack of masculine wisdom and our need for guidance towards real growth and maturity.

What we need, for ourselves and others in our lives, is the ability to honestly address our wounds and bring healthy closure to them.

3. Freedom from the dark heritage of the past. Moral guilt separates you from God. Secrecy isolates you from your spouse. Rigidity or laxness—both keep you from becoming a true moral leader with your children. These forces can be stopped so that the past loses its power over the present—and so you and your loved ones share a brighter future.

4. Help for beginning your life again. No, I'm not suggesting it will be quick and easy. But I'm confident that as you assimilate and live out the principles you're about to read, God will remake you from the inside out and guide you into the kind of spiritual manhood you want.

WHERE THIS PATH OF HEALING LEADS
What I'm inviting you to do is to take a "consequential journey."

Throughout this book we're going to look at the effects of abortion on your life—that is, the power this choice has had to shape you into the man you've become. Why do this? Because the most healing path is the one that causes us to look into the results of our own actions, then frees us to make new choices—to become greater, stronger men.

Along the way you'll have to face some deep fears—especially fears you were trying to avoid when you chose abortion as a quick way out. Why is this necessary? Because the very things we feared then are likely to be haunting us—and pouring spiritual toxins into our lives—today.

The most healing path is the one that causes us to look into the results of our own actions, then frees us to make new choices.

What I intend is to help guide you into the deepest healing of all: a spiritual relationship with God, a relationship that was seriously impaired when you went against him to end a life that he ordained. Many Christian men have a legal relationship with him in that they trust in the atoning sacrifice of Jesus Christ to remove the penalty of their sin and make them legally right in God's eyes. Others have an informational relationship with God, in which they study Bible doctrine and facts about him. Other guys relate to God's power, relying on him to answer prayers or give them supernatural gifts. But these relationships are not what I'm talking about.

I'm talking about a path of healing that can lead you into a relationship with God in which you know and experience his real presence in your life, a presence that can guide you in conscience, in the practical steps of daily living, and in meaningful service to God and others. I'm speaking of a full, true relationship in which you experience God as Sovereign and Lord, Father, mentor, confidant, friend—in short, a new way of knowing God that introduces you to the many aspects of who he is as a real, living being.

It is not God's will to punish you and abandon you to life as a fugitive. He invites you now to begin life anew, to let him restore a deep sense of well-being to your soul. He wants to assure you of his forgiveness, to provide loving discipline, to lead you on a path of healing that will redefine your life forever.

Isn't that the relationship with God you've always wanted?

THE BIG PAYOFF

I can assure you that facing the consequences of your choices is the right path to healing.

I can also assure you that you won't be on your own as you read. For one thing, you'll meet other men who have struggled with and faced the same issues you're facing. You will be guided through some action steps that will help you move toward growth as a man, husband, father, and Christian. You'll also be supplied with toll-free numbers that will put you in touch with trained counselors who can help you.

In the end, you can be reconnected with the man you were created to be: a man who has much more potential than you can imagine right now, and one who knows what it means to be a free, forgiven, maturing son of God.

Will you take this path? If you do so, wholeheartedly, you'll find that you no longer feel like a fugitive running from the past. You'll be amazed to discover that the choices that define you do not lie in the past but are just now opening up before you.

QUESTIONS

1. If you have had an abortion experience, explain how you felt after it was over. How do you feel about it now?
2. Which of the symptoms of the postabortive male in this chapter describe you today?
3. In what ways do you think the abortion has caused you to act as a "fugitive" running from the past? How do you feel inside when you act this way?
4. In what ways do you think the abortion experience has affected your general outlook on life? your self-image? your relationship with God? your relationship with others close to you?

Two

A World of Fugitives

A man's sexuality is one of the most powerful and important aspects of his life. If you don't think so, talk to guys whose sex drive has diminished due to an illness, or men who discover they're unable to father a child. We even joke about sex a lot, far more than women, but our jokes have a nervous edge.

Somewhere inside, most men ask themselves one of two questions. *Am I man enough?* Or *Am I still man enough?* Sexuality fuels our passions and can be the source of apprehension. The one thing that will scare a man into a doctor's office faster than anything else is a threat to his sexuality. We don't want to take any chances.

GAMBLING WITH SEXUALITY

While the physical dimensions of our sexuality command our attention, we remain generally clueless about the emotional and spiritual aspects of our sexual identity. Along the same lines, we often fail to make the connection between wrong sexual behavior and the negative consequences to our identity. Sex outside the shelter of marriage—whether in fantasy or in reality—means we lose the safe place where we can develop into the fullness of true manhood. Orgasm becomes auto-eroticism—for selfish gratification instead of relational intimacy. It dehumanizes our partner and it dehumanizes us as men. It destroys a union rather than builds it.

The ultimate consequence? We are meant, at orgasm, to bond with our partner. But if we view our partner as an object for pleasure—not a mate for life—we experience physical satisfaction but trigger a deeper need for fulfillment. We also gamble with one of our greatest potencies—our God-given power to contribute to the creation of life itself.

Some men have learned too late that an unwanted pregnancy and consequently abortion—the death of our own child—is the result of losing a sexual gamble. But what is it that causes men to gamble with sexuality in the first place—to have sex with women they're not committed to for life? Or to treat sex too casually, when they're not stupid and know full well that a baby, and weighty responsibilities, are at stake?

Gambling with our sexuality, treating it as a purely self-gratifying act, is a bad idea. In the end it drives us into emotional and spiritual isolation.

But we're not alone.

JON AND KEVIN. Carrying blankets and picnic coolers into the open-air jazz festival, Jon is glad he snagged four tickets for this sold-out event, one of the biggest on the West Coast. Kevin and his wife love jazz as much as Jon and his fiancée, Kristi, do.

Back in college Jon and his then-girlfriend had gone through two abortions before breaking up.

As the four of them settle on the lawn of the open-air amphitheater, with a great view of the stage, Jon thinks, *Maybe I should talk to Kevin sometime. He's a great guy. I could probably tell him what's bothering me.* But then he has second thoughts. *On the other hand, Kevin's a little too private. Almost secretive. I'm not sure what he'd think of me. But maybe that secretiveness is good. He'd keep his mouth shut. I need to figure out if I should tell Kristi before the wedding. . . .*

But as the festival amps up and the conversation mixes with music and relaxation, Jon changes his mind. *Kevin wouldn't understand. And I'm not even sure what a friend could do to help me anyway. Man, back then when I made the decision, I had no idea it would bother me so much now.*

Jon thinks Kevin is such a clean-cut guy. He can't recall Kevin even talking about women—or about his sexual exploits—like some of the other guys at work.

The ironic thing is that Kevin's also been keeping a secret. His wife, Terri, knows about other women in his past . . . but not about the summer during grad school when Kevin and his girlfriend conceived a child. He didn't have it in him to admit he had flown into a rage when the girl said she was pregnant and that he'd harassed her until she agreed to the abortion.

So Jon and Kevin each continue to live alone with their secrets—or so they think. Seated just forty feet away, the blond surfer-looking guy shares the same past. And so does the guy selling drinks at the concession stand. In fact, they are only four among many men—probably up to a quarter of the guys at the festival—who gave up the life of at least one child to abortion.

No, none of these guys is alone—at least not in the horrid action in which they participated. Since 1973, when abortion was legalized in the United States, some forty million babies have been lost to the procedure in hospitals and abortion clinics. Where are the fathers of these children? Odds are they're in any crowd you're in, living with the shame and isolating influences of a past abortion.

KYLE. Kyle enters the ski lodge at the end of a long, great day on the slopes and stows his snowboard at the valet service. Waiting around the fire are the other men and women who have all driven up together for a long weekend away from the New England college where they teach.

Late in the evening, talk moves from the latest music and movies to politics . . . and somehow to the issue of "choice." Suddenly the women are intense. Kyle is amazed at how open some of them are about their sex lives. Of the six, four speak frankly about having had an abortion. One guy, Jared, indirectly admits that one of his girlfriends had an abortion. Even though Jared tries to appear casual about it, Kyle thinks the splotches of embarrassment on his face tell a different story. The other guys just change the subject.

Kyle hates the feeling that comes over him. Even though he's read the statistics—1.4 million babies are aborted every year in the U.S. alone—why does the fact that there's an abortion in his past make him feel defective? It's not like he's especially religious or anything. So why does a voice tell him, *You didn't have enough guts to own up to your own child?*

Later, as he's drifting off to sleep, Kyle suddenly realizes there must be more than a few young men and women back at the college who have either chosen to abort a child or have contemplated doing it.

CLIFF. It's a muggy Friday evening in Dallas, and Cliff feels elated as he walks into the stadium with his teenage sons, Ben and Mark. He's never experienced anything like this massive gathering of men, all coming together for a summer weekend of worship, spiritual teaching, and prayer.

And the evening far exceeds his hopes. When the fifty thousand men rise from their seats to sing *Amazing Grace,* Cliff glimpses his young sons with their heads bowed in worship, and he chokes up. But he is far from feeling the deeply spiritual moment everyone around him seems to be experiencing. Deep in his soul there is only intense pain, remorse, and guilt.

If only . . . he thinks. Because one of his children is missing.

Later, the keynote speaker talks about sin—and about Jesus' blood sacrifice for every sin. But Cliff wonders: *every sin?* He looks around at the sincere faces, knowing these guys aren't super-saints. *But I'll bet very few of them paid to have their first child aborted, then lived for the next seventeen years pretending it never happened.*

His thoughts drift back to the year before he and Margie were married. Her parents were Christians, trying to talk her into dropping him because he was not a Christian at the time. "But he comes to church on Sunday evenings with me," Margie had argued in Cliff's defense. If her parents had known this was a cover for the fact they were having sex, they'd have booted him out of her life and packed her off to some Bible school that didn't even allow dating.

What Cliff would be shocked to know is that statistically, young men and women active in their Christian faith are almost as likely as the rest of the population to use abortion as a way out of an unplanned pregnancy.

In fact, a good percentage of the men he's staring at around this stadium—wondering what they'd think if they knew his hidden sin of abortion—are wondering the very same thing. Surprising as it seems, more than 50 percent of women getting abortions in the U.S. identify themselves as having conservative Christian affiliations.

If you factor in the potential grandparents and other relatives, virtually everyone in the church community is directly related to an aborted child . . . or knows someone who is.

I offer these statistics for several reasons.

First, it's important for every one of us to realize how vast and unchecked the crisis of abortion has become. Many recognize that abortion and its long-term effects are now epidemic. As much as abortionists insist we need abortion to be legal "in case a woman is raped or subject to incest," the facts show that approximately 98 percent of abortions are performed as a birth-control measure.

Second, I want you to see that you, as an abortive father, are not alone. A big problem for men is the silence they keep when it comes to some of life's most vital matters. Most men don't like to "make a big issue" of things, especially intimate matters. But in burying an event as enormous as an abortion, men sentence themselves to an isolation that keeps them from healing and moving on.

Most men don't like to "make a big issue" of things, especially intimate matters. But in burying an event as enormous as an abortion, men sentence themselves to an isolation that keeps them from healing and moving on.

As a result, many men go for years carrying a huge conflict inside. In order to live with themselves, men find some way to put a positive spin on an act they have never been able to truthfully justify. And all the while they know exactly what they're covering up.

What is it that men tell themselves to justify abandoning their own children through abortion?

"GOOD" REASONS FOR POOR CHOICES

Some want to paint the man who participates in abortion as a cold-hearted baby killer—a "casual inseminator" who has no concern for women or children at all. In part, it is this mentality that prevents a man from seeking help later, when the aftershocks of abortion may be shaking the foundations of his being. As a result, he is left on his own to look back helplessly and think, *What's wrong with me? How could I have been so cold?*

In fact, most men involved in abortion can honestly find some "good" reason for the choice they made—or what seemed like a good choice at the time. Couple that with the fact that most of us remain profoundly ignorant of the long-term impact of abortion, and it's easy to find at least one very "good" reason for a very poor choice.

Some guys, for example, see abortion as the way to right a wrong. Sure, men may see abortion as an unfortunate choice. But it can seem like the way to rectify a situation or a relationship that wasn't good in the first place.

For Marty, abortion seemed the right course when an unplanned pregnancy made him realize that he'd become too deeply tied to the wrong woman.

"The whole relationship with Alyson was bad from the start," he says. "I knew it. But the fact that we were having sex clouded the real issue.

"The truth is, all we did was fight. Alyson wasn't dealing with some really big emotional issues, and she was on a roller coaster all the time. I'm not saying everything was her fault. But it was a nightmare. We'd get together, have sex, fight and break up, then get back together. This went on for months. We were bad for each other. And I was too weak to end it."

When Alyson told Marty she was pregnant, there seemed only one good plan of action. "I believed having a child together was a very, very bad idea. I told myself it wasn't right to bring a child into the world under these circumstances. To me, terminating the pregnancy wasn't the greatest thing to do in itself, but it was a good way to end a bad relationship."

To Marty, emotional incompatibility with the child's mother seemed like a good reason to end their child's life.

Nick had other reasons to believe abortion was a good solution to a bad situation.

In fact, his girlfriend's mother made the choice to abort because Nick and Janet were both in high school. One evening Janet told him she'd missed her period. Just days later, in a single gut-wrenching phone call, she told him that she was pregnant and that her mother had scheduled her for an abortion. It was pretty much a done deal.

All Nick could do was try to find ways to tell himself it was for the best.

Most obvious was the fact that they were young and immature. He knew how difficult having a baby would be for two immature young people, unprepared as they were to carry the emotional burdens of parenthood. "I was kicking myself for being sexually active with her in the first place. We were just too young."

The truth is, even guys in their twenties and thirties often see abortion as a good way out, insisting they're "too immature" or "too young" to be fathers.

For Nick, there was another reason to cast the unhappy event in a better light. "I was a Christian and Janet wasn't. We didn't have the same spiritual beliefs or values." For a number of men, having different religious and spiritual backgrounds from the mother's is another plus in favor of an abortion.

A LIST AS LONG AS YOUR ARM
Men have a long list of other reasons for seeing abortion as the "right choice."

Kent told himself, *A baby should be born only to parents who love and want it—and we don't want a baby.*

Jeff rationalized, "I'm still in med school, advancing in my career. This is a terrible time for us to have a child."

Rob insisted, "She can't handle a baby right now. She's under too much stress."

Other guys rationalize:

- "When we can afford to [have her quit work or buy a house], we can have a baby."
- "We were being intimate, but she was trying to get back with her estranged husband." Or "I was trying to get back with my ex-wife."
- "Her family is really religious, and for us to have a baby out of wedlock would cause them pain and embarrassment."
- "Her father would kill her."
- "We hardly know each other."
- "She's the one responsible. She should have protected herself from pregnancy."
- "We don't want to get married. And growing up with a single mom, and a dad who's not around all the time, will be too hard on the baby."
- "Having the baby and giving it up for adoption would be too hard. The kid will always wonder where his real parents are. And we'd never be at peace knowing we have a child out there 'somewhere.' Why do that to anyone?"

THE TWO MOST COMMON REASONS
Of all the rationalizations men use to justify the decision to abort a child, I've found two to be the most prevalent.

Have you heard this one? Have you perhaps heard yourself saying it? "She's the one who'd have to go through pregnancy and childbirth. And she's not sure she wants the baby. Because I don't have to carry the baby, I don't have a right to tell her I want her to have it."

Frankly, this particular idea comes from the archfeminist rhetoric being promoted in our culture. It seems to offer a good reason for a man to concede to abortion—he's gallantly allowing the woman the right to sovereignty over her body. But it also relieves him of the proper sense of responsibility for the child he has fathered.

As Al puts it, "I didn't insist that my girlfriend [who later became Al's wife] keep the first baby because it was 'her body.' Later, after our first son was born, I didn't step in to help. I kept thinking, *If a baby is the property of the mother when it's in her womb, what's my responsibility for it outside the womb? Shouldn't [the baby's] personal care be the mother's responsibility? I guess I'm just supposed to provide the paycheck.*"

Which brings us to what I believe is the most common rationalization: "We were just having sex for fun." For single guys this comes out as, "We were just dating and having a good time." For married guys it's, "We didn't want a baby right now."

In either case, the thinking goes: "We were just enjoying the sex—a baby was never in the picture." That quite easily leads to thinking: *It's just tissue anyway.*

In other words, since you were treating sex as sport—purely as recreation—you weren't obligated to take its true power or its consequences seriously.

LIES . . . AND LONG-TERM CONSEQUENCES

No, men involved in abortion aren't heartless monsters. But they do have a big problem: With their justifications, "shading" of facts, and defensiveness, they have done violence to the truth—not to mention the violence they have done to themselves and their healthy spiritual growth.

Just reread the statements above. A clear-eyed look beneath the rhetoric reveals the manipulation of facts. Every reason given makes it sound as if someone is actually being protected— from something unbearable. Emotional upset. A life of reduced circumstances or lost dreams. Or from coming into this world with a less-than-ideal reception.

Nothing as profound as another person's life can be erased by reasoning it away. But by reasoning away the choice to end the life of a child, they set off down an unhealthy, even dangerous path. They learned to live parallel with reality, which eventually fragmented their personalities. To put it another way, distancing themselves from the truth about an abortion in their

lives continues to break their connection with real life, real
people, and real events. They continue to live apart from a
healthy sense of being, apart from having a place in the real
world. In the deepest way possible, they wind up with an
unmended heart, unable to connect with the people they now
want to love . . . and too proud to admit it.

If you've fathered an aborted child, you may recognize the
following scenario.

First, you experience an inability to connect emotionally
with reality. A friend stabs you in the back, and you shrug it
off. A parent or sibling contracts cancer, and you feel an eerie
indifference. Having steeled yourself against normal human
feelings in the face of a child's death by abortion, the numbness
slowly spreads. In time you grow dull to many of life's other
emotionally charged events.

As Jim says, "After a while, nothing fazed me anymore. Nothing got to me. My girlfriend would get emotional or upset, and
I'd just answer in a monotone. I told myself it was good to control my emotions. But nothing made me happy either. My
insides had withered and died." In the deepest sense, Jim's heart
was broken.

Next, you begin to feel closed in, existing in a private world,
disconnected from family or friends. You have the uncomfortable awareness that you are becoming very self-centered. Yet
you mostly respond to the joys, struggles, needs, and hurts of
others as intrusions that place unfair demands on you. ("Jill
had a severe migraine, so I had to do all her lousy work." Or
"Timmy had a high fever, and guess who got stuck in a hospital
room with him all weekend." Or "I can't stand it when Joe
cries. It makes me embarrassed and angry when my ten-year-
old acts like a baby.")

Having taken one serious step away from reality, you've
headed down the road of emotional paralysis—maybe even
emotional suicide. You slowly lose the ability to be intimately
linked to your own life . . . and you are too scared to regain a
rich connection with life by participating in the lives, loves,
needs, sorrows, and joys of others.

True, you may have set out to "right a wrong." But you have
given in to half-truths and reshaped reality around the lie. You
have failed to responsibly face and live with the full truth. The
moment you compromised and replaced the truth with a lie,
you took a sharp turn away from the path of adult, emotional
maturity.

Why?

Emotional maturity comes only as we learn to deal with the
full truth—not just the parts that are easy or that benefit us, but
the parts that challenge, stretch, and force us to grow. Adulthood, in spiritual terms, comes as we face and make choices
that are best for everyone involved, even if those benevolent
choices cost us something. Our adult character grows when
we realize that, yes, we made some poor initial choices . . . and
now we can and must accept responsibility and do the right
thing to correct those mistakes.

Growing to maturity is about making positive choices no
matter where you find yourself right now. As spiritual men,
we know there is no way we can do this apart from God's help.

LEAVING ADOLESCENCE BEHIND

The truth is, for many men, choosing abortion was an "easy"
payment for a sexual high. It was the way to remain in a world
where actions didn't have consequences or demand much—
a fantasy world of boyhood and adolescence.

This is why most postabortive men experience some sense of
uncertainty and questions about manhood. What is masculine
wholeness? What is manly character? How does a man deal with
the emotional variety and challenge of life?

- A man *learns to grapple with the emotions and stresses and joy and
  exasperation of living with a real flesh-and-blood woman;* an adolescent
  *escapes into a dreamworld of flawlessly beautiful women who do everything
  he wants.* That, of course, is the appeal of pornography,
  which offers empty satisfaction to that hollow fear that we
  may be undesirable and rejected—and to the fear that we're
  powerless to sustain the interest of a good woman. But

pornography never fulfills the sexual man; it only tempo-
rarily and shallowly gratifies his selfish desire to experience
a release *of sexual tension.*

- A man *engages with children and can see the world from their incomplete,
  inexperienced viewpoint, enabling him to teach and coach and mentor by
  filling in the blanks; an* adolescent *is annoyed, made impatient, or
  embarrassed by childish mess-ups.* If we're childish in emotional,
  spiritual, and real-life matters, we cannot offer mature
  wisdom and understanding to our sons and daughters.
  Participating in abortion can block the confidence it takes
  to make the transition from boyish selfishness to manly
  self-giving.

- A man *listens, even if he doesn't like it, to see if his critic has a good point;
  an* adolescent *can't tolerate even a hint that he's wrong.* Without
  confidence in our personal worth, we will always feel
  compelled to defend when we should listen—to win the
  imagined "battle" to prove we are worthy.

- A man *thinks through his fears, understands what he may gain and lose
  by dealing responsibly with a challenge, then shoulders responsibility—
  win, lose, or draw.* This describes the struggle of emotional
  growth and what it takes to make the difficult passage to
  mature adulthood. It's the transition every male must
  make if he wants to leave behind the emotional adolescent and become a man.

> **Participating in abortion can block the confidence it takes to make the transition from boyish selfishness to manly self-giving.**

Wrestling through tough decisions,
accepting responsibility for ourselves and
others, living with the consequences of
long-term commitment, learning that
fathering is far more than siring or just
providing cash . . . these are the things
that make a man.

It's time for men to look squarely at how
abortion has *really* affected them—at the
deepest levels of their being. A child paid
with his or her life for the father's sexual
pleasure—and for his freedom to remain
in a fantasyland without responsibility. Post-

abortive men didn't know that this fantasyland is a theme park for the emotionally and spiritually disabled. And though admission is free, there is a very costly exit fee no one told them about. Ironically, men go on paying the price for years—at the cost of a stable and healthy manhood.

How do men pay? They pay with a deep sense of shame when they'd love nothing better than to feel clean and not stained or defective before God. They pay with years of guilt when they'd love to feel worthy around women and children. They pay in their efforts to measure up when they're around "decent" men whose brotherhood they'd like to share.

THE INVISIBLE CAGE

As a postabortive man, you may sometimes feel as if you're stuck inside invisible bars. By that I mean you may find symptoms like these wreaking havoc in your life, holding you back when other men seem to move on, grow, and find fulfillment:

1. **Relationship struggles.** Things may go great at first—then you hit a snag. Quite likely, it's the same issue that derails the relationship with the woman in your life every time.

2. **Inability to trust friends.** Your critical eye spots their flaws in a heartbeat, and you can find a list of reasons *not* to seek or trust their advice. You may push friends away because, in some way, they let you down just about every time. Or on the other hand, they may be too friendly and then discover your secret.

3. **Rage.** In fact, you don't have to be an explosive tyrant for rage to control you. You may be Mister Nice Guy most of the time—just as surprised by your sudden nuclear attacks as the people you crush.

4. **Addictions.** We don't master the crummy parts of reality, we mostly escape them. Alcohol, drugs . . . these are ways we avoid facing the fears and deficits we meet in ourselves when life slams us into its tougher realities.

5. **Sexual compulsions.** Many postabortive men find themselves trapped in patterns that make them feel degraded. They

may become involved in an illicit relationship, which they later
have to betray . . . and then quickly move on. Or they may
compartmentalize their promiscuity, indulging in pornography
or "renting sex" *only* when they're out of town on business.
These compulsions make them feel reduced, like weak and silly
adolescents.

Symptoms You May Have

> Relationship struggles
> Inability to trust friends
> Rage
> Addictions
> Sexual compulsions

Additional Behavioral Clues

> Sleeplessness, bad dreams, nightmares
> Sexual dysfunctions
> Depression, fear of failure, fear of rejection
> Loneliness or numbness

THE NEW DAY

Many postabortive men get tired of the fantasyland they're
stuck in and become desperate or disgusted enough to seek
help. They want life to change. Some find counselors and
start down the right path, only to quit after a few weeks. Why?
Because they see that, in order for life to be different, *they* will
be required to change at a profound level. And they're either
unwilling to change or they give in to a despairing voice that
whispers, *You can't change. You're damaged goods.*

A guy who gives up on counseling may feel like the convict
who's tunneled his way out of prison to daylight, only to stare
up into the muzzle of a gun. All that effort ending in dismal
defeat . . . and the conviction that he can run all he wants but
he'll never escape himself.

Perhaps the biggest factor that keeps men from finding the

help they need is that most of them don't know *how* to get help—
especially from other men who could give them wisdom and
guidance on these defining issues of manhood. You'd think it
would be the most natural thing in the world, but it's not. The
main reason men don't know how to find good help is crucial—
in fact, it lies at the root of the problem and at the head of the
path to healing, growth, and freedom. This fundamental issue
is the focus of our next chapter.

For now, I can assure you of one thing. When a man makes a
commitment to seek help resolving his own issues with the past,
it's a new day. A brand-new future starts to
unfold for him.

As we close this chapter, let me ask: Are
you tired of the prison of shame and guilt?
Tired of feeling driven, of doing things
that make you feel more like an out-of-
control adolescent than a real man? Isn't it
time to stop paying penalties for the past?

Before you do anything else, please
pause *right now* and make a new commitment
before God. Pray and ask for his help to
boldly face the real issues going on inside
you. Ask God for strength to seek help and
counsel and to stay committed to it even
when you want to give up. Give God charge
of everything in your whole life—even your
weakness and failures.

> **When a man makes a commitment to seek help resolving his own issues with the past, it's a new day. A brand-new future starts to unfold for him.**

When you pray this prayer, you release
the greatest force a man can know—the power of God working
in your own mind, will, and emotions. It's a power that will
begin to remake you from the inside out as the new man you
want to become.

As I said, there is an exit fee to escape the theme park of
unreality and adolescence. But the good news is that outside,
in the world of growing masculine maturity, you get to live
the real life you've been wanting.

In the next chapter we'll look at the cost of avoiding spiritual and emotional manhood, as well as the benefits of making healthy new choices.

QUESTIONS

1. When you participated in abortion, did you think of it as "birth control"? Or was it something more? Have your thoughts changed since? If so, in what ways?
2. Whose stories in this chapter did you identify with most? Why?
3. How have your thoughts changed over time regarding the connection between sex and true manhood?
4. As you've read the first two chapters, what thoughts or convictions do you think God is beginning to place on your heart? How do you think he wants you to respond?
5. Did you pray the suggested prayer at the end of this chapter? If not, don't put it off any longer—take a few minutes right now. If you prayed the prayer, what assurance from God can you now claim for the future?

Three

The Heart of the Matter

Why do men run from healthy manhood?

Running away from something so good doesn't make sense, does it? Nonetheless, it's precisely what many of us do—especially the postabortive man. We've looked briefly at the costs men pay for detouring, such as taking the path of least resistance and avoiding responsibility. The thing is, it's easy to get accustomed to life in Extended Adolescence Land.

Brent isn't thrilled with the fact that he feels disqualified from taking any leadership in his church. But labeling himself unfit for spiritual leadership leaves him free to build his own business and pursue hobbies he likes.

Andy doesn't like the fact that his wife's fears govern most of their decisions—about investments, job changes, the kids. But letting her emotions take the lead keeps him from having to feel bad if he were to challenge her or to risk taking charge when he believes she's wrong.

Jerry knows he isn't the greatest dad in the world, as he devotes all his energy to his produce business. He can run a business but hates it when his kids ask him a question about some moral matter such as premarital sex. He feels neither comfortable nor qualified to discuss such issues, especially with his children.

Ducking the responsibility for growth in masculinity—which includes leading in relationships—does have its perks. But that's just one reason why many men missed the turn on the highway—the one with the sign that said, Adulthood and Maturity—Turn Here.

WHERE DID ALL THE ADULTS GO?

There is a popular movie, a suspense chiller, in which the children in a certain rural town disappear one by one. The haunting question that sets the tone is, Where did all these kids go?

Most men could ask a similar question: Where did the adult males go—the men who could have shown us how to negotiate those challenges in the road that would have led us into healthy, mature manhood?

> **Adulthood is, in part, about making choices. More than that, it's about learning how to live with the results of your choices.**

Adulthood is, in part, about making choices. More than that, it's about learning how to live with the results of your choices. In a real sense, adulthood means *owning* what your choices have bought you—recognizing that, at best, the decisions you make are always going to be a mixture of good and bad, win and lose.

A guy I know likes to buy good used cars and keep them going for years. Dave's mechanic keeps telling him to put his money into a new car. "You keep paying to repair this one every few months," he points out.

But Dave insists, "Even with the repairs, it's still a lot cheaper than buying another car. And I like this car—problems and all." Dave is willing to own, literally, the bad with the good. So he keeps working on his old car and learning how to make it run right—a healthy attitude if keeping an old car is your choice.

Adulthood is about making choices. It's about taking on the risky, uncertain business of living and learning from the consequences of our choices. This requires being truthful about all that we don't know. Only an adolescent holds onto the self-protective illusion that he doesn't need help because, after all, he knows everything—right?

CATCH-22

This is where postabortive men often encounter a classic catch-22. Facing tough decisions, making choices, and owning the consequences of those choices is a big part of coming to maturity and growing into manhood. But besides pretending that they don't need help, they also carry on with the fantasy that their choices have no up-front or back-end cost. (Maybe that's why we're a nation of debtors.) And every time a man fails to face and work through consequences, something very strong and masculine in him atrophies a little more.

Another problem is the mind-set that no sacrifice someone else has to make for my convenience is too great. If a baby can give its life so I don't have to be bothered with the responsibilities of fathering and relationship, why shouldn't I expect that others will always fix problems for me at their expense?

For postabortive men who have yet to fully work through the consequences of ending a life, there's still a long stretch of road ahead on the way to mature adulthood. They've failed, so far, to work through a deeply complicated issue. When it comes to working through consequences—let alone facing them—they're pretty unclear on how to do it.

THE HEART OF THE MATTER

When it comes to our growth to responsible manhood, there's one major issue we have to face: A boy can raise a dog, a steer, a horse. *It takes a man to raise a man.* And few of us have had men in our lives to take the lead and show us the way to mature manhood.

Who were the role models in your life—men who led not just in words, but by example? Who showed you how to handle consequences—not just in small matters but in big ones? Where are the men in your life *today* who allow you to get close enough to see the failures and successes that are a necessary part of learning about matters such as male sexuality or manhood?

Few men have male relationships that show them what emotional depth and strength look like. And when it comes to matters of sexuality? Other than one uncomfortable adolescent talk about sex with their dads—if that—few men have male friends or relatives they feel comfortable talking to about such deeply personal matters.

One of the unwritten rules of manhood, it seems, is this: Just don't talk about it—especially the stuff that makes you uncomfortable. We've been taught to think that showing lack of knowledge about maleness reveals us to be stupid, naïve, weak, and unsafe. We'd rather pretend that we are mature and "in the know" than let anybody know we have questions. Most of us picked up these attitudes right at home, from the very first man we ever knew and looked up to. Consider the matter of our sexuality.

Rich was only sixteen when his mother and father came home early from a shopping trip one afternoon and caught him and his girlfriend sexually involved on the sofa. Later, his dad came to his room—sent by Rich's mom because this was obviously a man's job.

Rich still recalls his dad's red face and how his voice cracked as he spoke. "You don't need to do that sort of thing, Son."

"Okay," Rich replied, staring at the floor.

A long pause, then his dad went on awkwardly. "Your mother's very upset. We're moral people. We raised you to be moral."

"I know," Rich agreed. He'd been taught not to lie, steal, or punch. But he couldn't remember a word about sex.

"And you don't want to become a father at sixteen, do you?"

"No."

"Good," his dad finished, letting out a relieved breath. "Then don't do anything like that again. And you'd better stay away from that girl from now on. I'm sure there are a lot of nice girls in your class."

When Rich came out of his room later, his mom was putting dinner on the table and his dad was reading the paper. "The little upset was over," says Rich. "The surface was smooth again. No one ever brought it up after that."

Adam's dad was the just the opposite of Rich's father. While

Rich's dad was mild mannered, Adam's father blew up over everything.

"Dad caught me drinking, smoking, and lying. Every time, I knew what was coming. He'd scream and yell. When he suspected I was sleeping with Gail, he was so mad that he slammed me into the wall."

What did these two fathers teach their sons about responsible sexuality? And about life?

"I got the message," says Rich, "that upsetting my parents was the real problem. As long as everything was kept pleasant on the surface, your real behavior didn't matter. No one talked to me about how to control my sex drive or about the whys of sexual responsibility. No one taught me anything about maturity. It was just assumed that I'd 'be good' so Mom wouldn't be upset. I was left with these immature ideas about sex . . . and I just decided to start using condoms to be safe. Mostly I got better at hiding what I was doing."

Adam says, "The message I got was that it's a man's right to blow up, lose control, and force everybody to do what you want. What did my father teach me about self-control or sex or what it means to be a mature adult? Are you kidding?"

When it comes to one of the most central matters in our lives, most of us men were trained poorly, or not at all, by men who were themselves poorly equipped to prepare us for the road ahead.

ABANDONED IN THE BATTLE

Sex is one of the most potent forces in a man's life. One writer referred to it as a man's "center of gravity." If a guy is sick or injured but can still function sexually, he jokes with some relief, "At least *that's* still working!"

But sexual impulses and sexual relationships are also the source of a lot of conflict and questioning for us. When all that energy is at work, and at the same time we're entering unknown territory, sexuality is also the source of a lot of instability. We're stumbling along through a minefield—unsure but driven to move forward.

Growing into sexual maturity happens best in an environ-
ment that's emotionally stable, where people are committed
to each other. Sexual energy needs grounding.

Unfortunately, many of us today didn't have the grounding
of a stable home life. The present generation is the first in history to see an epidemic of divorce, abuse, and abandonment.
And we're just now beginning to feel the effects of this social
earthquake. This is what we do know:

- Fifty to 67 percent of first marriages end in divorce. When
  it comes to second marriages, 80 percent are likely to
  dissolve.[1] This, added to other social factors, means that . . .
- the United States now leads the world in fatherless
  families.[2]
- Since the most significant factor in a boy's life—shaping his
  masculine identity in profound ways—comes from having a
  close relationship with his father, what effect does so much
  upheaval have on boys as they grow to manhood? To put it
  more directly, what was the potential impact on *you*, if you
  grew up in a home without a nurturing dad?

A ten-year study of sixty families that went through divorce
drew a number of sad conclusions. Here are just a few that men
need to think about:

- When fathers moved out of the house, the relationship with
  their children eroded significantly. (The relationship
  deteriorated even more if one or both parents remarried.)
- As much as ten years after the divorce, children still felt
  "less protected, less cared for, less comforted." They
  carried vivid "gut-wrenching" memories of their parents'
  separation, even into adulthood.
- For boys, the effects of losing close, daily contact with
  their dads were somewhat severe. Preadolescent boys
  showed "an intense longing for their fathers" that seemed
  "physically painful." Not only did their need for their
  dads' guiding presence and influence continue, it *grew more*

intense in their teenage years . . . and became even more
acute when it was time to leave home.[3]

Obviously, when fathers move out, it's a problem that affects
their daughters as well as their sons.

- Even girls from advantaged backgrounds are *five times more likely*
to become teen mothers if they grow up in homes without
their fathers around than if they grow up in homes with both
biological parents.[4]

What's the most significant social problem in America, con-
tributing to financial, emotional, and even mental instability?
According to a Gallup poll, almost 80 percent of Americans
insist it is "the physical absence of a father in the home."[5]

Fathers are abandoning their place in their children's lives
through divorce. When that happens, the stable ground young
people need to make a solid launch into adulthood crumbles
beneath their feet. And stability is what we need to face the
choices and consequences of manhood, or else we will return
again and again to a mushy fantasyland of our boyhood, where
demands and unhappy endings are only a happy blur.

EVERY MAN NEEDS TO BE FATHERED

Not every one of us lost our access to dad because of divorce.
Having a father move out is only one way to lose touch with
his guidance and experience. Far more of us just never had
access to what our dads could have taught us about life. Many
of our fathers didn't communicate. They were preoccupied
with work, or they were ill prepared for or unaware of their
mandate to nurture their growing sons, or they kept us at a
distance because we were "just boys" who didn't belong in
their world.

It's also true that your father might have been a great guy
and treated you well—but he failed to teach you certain
important aspects of adult living. Carl's dad, for example,
was a financial wizard, "but he never taught me a thing about

handling money. My financial mistakes have caused me a lot of grief."

A man's job in fathering doesn't end at conception. That's called "siring." And it doesn't end after a man's sons are through peewee baseball and in-line hockey, or after they've chosen a college and career path. Boys need the wisdom and training of caring men in every area of life. They need to be fathered.

To father means to sign on for a lifetime of living, learning, and passing down to our sons (and daughters) what we have learned about the road that still lies ahead of them. We show them the way by passing on wisdom and insight. We explain why standards, rules and laws, customs and traditions are right and good. We give up-close guidance and direction without judging or belittling. In the past, this aspect of fathering was shared by men other than fathers—like granddads, uncles, or even brothers who were much older—because it's a huge job for any one man.

> **Boys need the wisdom and training of caring men in every area of life. They need to be fathered.**

For several generations, though, men have just not been around. True, some men today are working hard to restore better contact with their children—caring for them as babies, coaching them as they grow, opening up conversation. But that kind of conscientious fathering wasn't there for many of us. Or else our parents divorced, and seeing dad at all was crammed into a weekend or part of a single day. As for help from extended family, that hardly happens anymore, as families and old friends sprawl apart from each other across the map.

Men who take seriously the charge of raising young men to adulthood are few and far between. Countless men who feel lost in the middle of manhood will attest to that.

Bottom line: Many postabortive men acknowledge that the men who could have influenced them on important life issues—especially in the area of sexuality—did not take on the responsibility.

SPEAK UP

Here are some of the matters postabortive men wish their
fathers, or other men important to them, had discussed:

1. **Sexuality.** Many men say they got "the talk," in some form
or other, from their fathers. But for most the atmosphere was
uncomfortable—even clinical.

"When it was over," says Paul, "I could tell my father was
relieved. He couldn't get out of the room fast enough. There
was nothing in his manner that invited me to come back to him
with any questions. I don't know if I would have, but the door
sure wasn't left open."

Morris recalls, "My father asked me to tell him what I'd
learned about sex in health class. I got a little tongue-tied. So
he'd say, 'Did they tell you this? Did they tell you this?' I'd nod
or say 'Uh-huh.' He just patted me on the shoulder and said,
'That's good. I'm glad you know this now.'"

Frankly, the lack of open communication about basic sexuality is appalling. Yes, it's true that some of our discomfort on
this very personal matter is probably natural and good. But
when a father bails out of his responsibility to pass healthy sexual
knowledge on to his son, he, in effect, tosses his son to the
wolves who print pornography and make R-rated movies. Or he
leaves his son in the hands of other misinformed adolescents.

2. **Sexual ethics.** How far is too far? When is it not okay to
be alone with a girl? When a girl says no, does she really *mean*
no? If you're in love and you *know* you're going to get married,
is sex okay? If you do a girl a favor, does she owe you something
in return? Can't you convince a girl it's right by forcing yourself on her just a little?

Many of us were confused on these points when we were
younger. When did any older male help sort out our thinking?
For most of us the answer is, "The day pigs flew."

Bob says, "My parents had a frank discussion with me about
sex when I was fourteen. At least about the mechanics." But
he still had a lot of questions about the situations in which he
found himself. And he had buddies who, naturally, also were
confused about the subtleties of relationships.

"My Sunday school teacher was a great guy. He knew that most of us were really confused about relationships and sex. So one Sunday he segregated the class—boys in one room and girls in another—and talked straight talk. It wasn't graphic. It was just honest talk about pressure and manipulation and the importance of not 'using' others. He talked to us about our responsibility."

Unfortunately, the repercussions were swift and strong. "This was a very conservative, Bible-preaching church," Bob remembers. "I came to Christ when I was nine, got baptized at age ten, and went to all the youth functions. We were big on spiritual things but not so great on life issues. When the adults found out this guy had talked to us about sexual responsibilities, they were very unhappy. The pastor and elders shut the class down, and the teacher was kicked out of the position."

The truth is, in Bob's church a spiritual community of men bailed out on their responsibility to educate young people about sexual ethics and identity. By shutting down open discussion of issues that confuse many adults—let alone teenagers—these men gave up a tremendous opportunity to mentor a whole group of young men- and women-in-the-making.

"Much later," Bob adds, "when I was separated from my wife and working in the movie industry in Hollywood, I know I was vulnerable because I hadn't thought through sexual issues. Now here I was in the middle of a world of men and women throwing themselves at each other. I was much more susceptible to the influences of the crowd I was running with—even though I was an adult—than I would have been if an adult had helped me think through issues of sexual responsibility early on."

3. Consequences of sexual behavior. Young males are not noted for their tendency to think through the consequences of their actions. The only thing we had in mind as we climbed to the top of the bridge was what a rush it was going to be jumping into the river. The adrenaline rush was the thing.

And when it came to how our actions and words affected other people—*what* other people? How much time did you spend, as a young guy, thinking how a girl would feel if you

took her out, didn't like her, and dropped her without a word?
Our self-centeredness was unchallenged. And frankly, for
many men it remains a problem far into adulthood.

As boys, we needed guidance to understand there would be
definite consequences of our actions and our attitudes. But
did we get it?

In some cases the guidance we got only emphasized the
negative: "If you get a girl pregnant, you'll have a big load
of responsibility, and you don't want that." "You'll have to
give up your dreams and become a nine-to-five drudge."
"You'll kill all your options." "You might get a serious dis-
ease."

The philosophy behind this approach seemed to be, "Make
it look really bad and you'll scare them away from sexual
activity."

This ignores the fact that a young man will become sexually
active someday—whether it's just in holding a girl for the first
time and feeling a wild electricity run through him, or after
he's made a lifetime commitment to her. Yes, young men need
to have someone help them set strong boundaries for their
sexual potency. But along with that they need positive, appro-
priate training at every step as sexual magnetism becomes a
force in life. The very reason some of you are reading this book
is because you participated in conceiving a child before anyone
had given you positive guidance about what to do if you should
find yourself in that situation. At a moment of crisis and instability—with maximum potential to do the self-centered thing
that would hurt someone else—you had to come up with your
own solution.

For some guys, guidance came from women and had a femi-
nist color: "A man should always support a woman's choice
because she has the most responsibility in bearing and raising
a child." And the message may have had a bigoted slant: "Men
like to dump responsibility on women and come and go as they
please."

There are really two negative attitudes at work here.

The first sends this message: Because a child comes from

a woman's body and she may care for its infant needs more than a man, fathers have less right to make choices about their children.

The second attitude says: Men are a subspecies you just can't count on.

Underneath it all, there seems to lie a more basic—and tragic—attitude: Males are just not good at relationships, so why bother to train them much at all? Just teach guys to be competitive and strong, and let women take the lead in home *and family matters.*

WHO SHOWS YOU THE WAY?
I want to return to the question I posed earlier. If it's true that every one of us still needs the wisdom and training of men who are ahead of us on the trail of manhood, then who are the men showing you the way?

We need help with the healthy disciplines that make a man. The ability to commit ourselves to the right thing *when commitment is costly* is not a trait found in human nature. When you do find it in a man, you find it was built into him by his family, his religion, or some other force that intentionally shaped his masculine side during his emotional and spiritual formation.

We do need the help of other men who will help "father" our spirit in the right ways. We already have proof of our need: Left to find our way into the unknown forest of sexuality, using the light of our own wisdom, we tripped up. Choosing fatherhood, with its great challenges and rewards, would have begun to transform us from fantasy-driven, escapist adolescents into solid and stable men. Instead, many men chose the "easy," "convenient" way out.

Sexuality is a state of being, and being sexual is a pattern of behavior with eternal consequences. Our power to procreate is the blessing of God. Using that power in a godly way is the success of manhood, fatherhood, and husbandhood. Sexual purity and commitment are so important to God that he promises he will bless those who keep pure sexually.

Spiritual manhood begins with humility, because humility was a central character trait of Jesus Christ (see Philippians 2). Jesus lowered himself and became one of us so he could learn firsthand what it means to be a male in human flesh. Humility, for us men, means that we stop projecting an image that we're greater than we are. We stop pretending that we're superior in our knowledge, achievements, and character in order to impress other people and fool ourselves. We start admitting we're in need of help, training, and direction in many areas, including responsible, mature male sexuality.

GOOD QUESTIONS

Let me ask you several direct questions. Please don't skip through them. Ponder them carefully because they can help put you on the road to recovery from the devastating effects of your past.

Are You Willing to Admit That You Need Help?

I'm not talking just at this moment, but throughout your life, in order to continue growing as a healthy man? For some of us, two of the most difficult hurdles to jump are formed by the words *I need your help* and *I don't know.* In our eyes, admitting need is a sign of weakness.

Frankly, it's time to get over that. Continuing to live in need and lack of knowledge is what truly keeps us weak, when getting resources from other men could make us strong. It's harder to build a great investment portfolio if you won't ask for help from people who know investments better than you do. And it's much tougher to grow as a man if you won't seek wisdom and know-how about life from men more mature than you.

Commit today to be honest with yourself about your constant need for help and guidance from wise, spiritually mature men.

Who Can You Talk to about Your Guilt and Sense of Shame?

This may be an even tougher issue for most men. Some of

us would take a beating with a stick before admitting we've done wrong. Our pride—mixed with shame and maybe self-loathing—runs deep.

But we do make mistakes. We sin. And if we don't know how to deal with the guilt, we're left thinking we're defective and unworthy. This cuts us off from God and from other people who need us. As we noted earlier, lingering guilt and shame tell us we have no right to lead other people, especially in moral issues.

Who can you talk to honestly and confess what you've done? Who can you listen to—someone who won't merely sympathize or excuse what you've done but will also help you understand how to make things right and encourage you to follow steps that lead to change?

Obviously, I can't direct you specifically in whom to go to, since I have no knowledge of the men in your specific world. But here are some guidelines to consider as you seek out someone—a spiritual mentor—who can help you grow into your full masculine identity:

- *He should be a man who is humble, a man at peace with himself and with you.* Beware of someone who tries to impress you. If he appears to find his identity in what he does—his work success, other accomplishments, or the act of being a great husband or a great dad—he may be prone to giving superficial formulas for self-improvement. He may see you as another project—something he can fix.

You need to find a mature friend who accepts himself and accepts *you* as you are. Someone who is willing to come alongside you and be delighted when you reach personal break-throughs—without claiming them to his credit. His humility will show in that he is comfortable with his strengths even as he acknowledges his limitations and his own susceptibility to temptation and sin.

He should be a good listener who helps you put your deepest struggles and joys into words. He should have the ability to gently correct a "diseased" perception you may have about yourself, someone else, or your situation.

- *He should be a man who doesn't "need to be needed."* People will sometimes want to be needed by someone else who's needy because of hidden and unresolved brokenness in their own lives. He may be good at understanding your pain but lack the maturity—in terms of emotional and spiritual resources—needed to help you grow. He can give you only what he himself has learned to receive from God, even though it may not be what you need.

Need cannot minister to need. A guy like this may be trying to earn points with God by helping you, or he may be getting a voyeuristic thrill from observing the stuff you're struggling with instead of dealing with his own issues.

A guy who is in this place will tend to exert negative control over you or will get in the way of your personal development. He can't guide or encourage you on a journey he hasn't taken himself.

- *He should be comfortable with keeping confidences . . . and committed to it on principle.* A man who reveals sensitive matters about someone else or who criticizes other people behind their backs should be avoided. You need the freedom to talk about critical areas of your life, to ask embarrassing and revealing questions, to admit things that you're ashamed of or that you've done wrong. That requires a safe relationship with a man you can trust.

A man who typically honors confidences will speak well of others and will provide that safe place you need in order to be open . . . which will lead you to forgiveness, healing, and mature growth in masculinity.

- *He should draw his strength and sense of direction from God . . . and encourage you to do the same.* If a man observes a regular disci-

pline of studying God's Word and praying, he is more likely
to have access to the supernatural resources—such as grace,
patience, and firm love—needed to help you grow.

Doesn't it make sense that you should be in a relationship with
someone who knows the One who is the source of power for
healthy spiritual growth?

- *He should be a man who has suffered well and struggled well with loss
  and personal sin.* The man you seek should be the kind
  of guy who has come to understand godly sorrow and
  the conviction that leads to positive character development and a fuller life. He will stand in contrast to
  someone who wallows in suffering or who seeks to deaden
  unresolved pain through work, alcohol, drugs, or other
  destructive means.

The man you find may not have gone through the abortion
experience. That's not necessary. Every one of us has suffered in
some way. It is necessary, though, to interact with someone who
has learned to do more than survive. Look for someone who has
learned to live in the fullness of God's love.

In short, the characteristics you're looking for in a personal
mentor are exactly the characteristics that *you* want to develop
yourself. As you are forgiven and set free from the past, you
will find yourself growing in these godly character traits and
becoming the man God designed you to be. We will look more
closely at this important matter of finding a spiritual mentor
in a later chapter. But for now, if you can readily think of a
man whose advice you'd seek and whose accountability you'd
welcome, that's great. Make a commitment to get together with
him regularly. Or maybe you need to begin today to search
for someone you can trust to keep confidential what you need
to get off your chest and to give you sound advice. I strongly
encourage you to do so.

It is possible that you will not run into one man who exhibits
all these characteristics. They are rare. It is worth the search

though. And in a very important way your willingness to hunt out the right man to help is actually a fundamental first piece of your move toward wholeness. You have to engage your will. Set aside discouragement, disappointment, hopelessness, laziness—all in the effort to begin to help yourself. The word is *determination.* Eventually, your determination to find a geniune mentor, is going to pay off.

On the way, though, you may also find various men who are, like you, looking for honesty, a safe atmosphere in which to know and be known, support *and* challenge to grow. No one of them may fit the mentor "bill," but they can become true spiritual brothers to you. And a man needs these on the road to wholeness and spiritual manhood. Enjoy what you can in the various honest seekers you will meet along the way. Value them. Support them, and ask for such support as they can give. They are also gifts of gold to you.

Who Can You Talk to about Sex?

Is it just the guys in the locker room? Like so many men, you may have had to figure out sex on your own. Few of us can say we learned about real sex or sexual identity from an adult male who cared about our physical and spiritual well-being. And few of us can say we have even a single friend or older male to whom we would go *today* with questions about sex.

Unfortunately, the message many of us got from absent or silent males was that talking to another man to get information of a sexual nature is not something you do. As if a real man just knows these things without asking.

The physical act of sex—and how it relates to our emotional and spiritual makeup—will present questions to us our whole lives. That's because sex is connected to so many related issues in a man's life, including aging, health, and emotional needs such as our sense of attractiveness and worth. Our need for sexual information didn't end when we figured out what to do on the honeymoon.

Who would you go to to get a healthy, wise perspective on sex and sex-related matters? Without someone to ask, we're alone

with our anxieties when we don't have to be. We men need to
overcome the male legacy of awkwardness and silence in matters
relating to sex—to be free to seek answers to our questions
throughout life.

Who Influences Your Attitudes about Sex?

Along with the basic facts about sex, you and I got a lot of mes-
sages from men, and each one conveyed someone's attitude:

- "A man controls the sexual event, gets the woman to do
  what he wants."
- "A man has more needs than a woman can fulfill, so he
  needs other outlets."
- "Sex is just something you enjoy."

These and other wrong attitudes about sex heavily influence
men's thinking. As we think, so we behave.

Are there men you know who have both healthy and godly
attitudes about sex? You need the influence of their better
thinking to help counteract the poor, low, and immoral attitudes that bombard us all every day.

Who Shapes Your View of Yourself and Your Spiritual Role in the Lives of People You Love?

As we saw before, postabortive men feel as if they've given up
the right to be positive leaders and role models. They feel
marked, reclassified, and disqualified: "Better to keep my head
low when it comes to leadership and moral authority—I don't
want to be a hypocrite."

Some of this thinking comes from a right and God-given
recognition of the sin and guilt that drives anyone to seek
God's forgiveness. Unfortunately, legalistic thinking can persist
long after we've been forgiven. Even more unfortunate is that
some of us attend churches that preach sin and the law more
than they preach God's grace—grace that not only releases us
from the past but also empowers us to become new men for
today and for the future.

In becoming new men before God, we stop listening to past assessments of ourselves and stop accepting past limitations on what we are to do with our lives. We start listening to God and obeying his directions for us. We stop saying "I'm not able" because God says to us, "I will give you the strength, vision, and wisdom, and you will be able."

Yes, a big part of your life—positive leadership—was killed along with your child. But it can be resurrected. You can be restored to a place of responsible spiritual leadership. Make no mistake, this is God's will for every one of us.

THE RESTORER OF LIFE

Although the men in your life may have left you to find your way alone, God does not. He wants to renew his relationship with you—a relationship that will heal and transform your core identity. God is extending his personal invitation: "My son, you're no longer a fugitive. Stop running, and let me cleanse you from the past by restoring a right spirit in you" (see Psalm 51).

Something deep in the spirit of a postabortive man needs to be "refathered"—brought to life. The death of your child brought death to your spirit. Only the One who is Life can give a new life to you.

How does God restore life where there has been death? I can best explain with an example. Some men train their sons to be responsible for what they own by helping them develop good stewardship habits—for instance, washing the car every weekend, storing their bike inside instead of leaving it out in the elements, cleaning their shoes, taking care of their clothes. Their fathering "patterns" into their sons a lifelong habit of responsibility with possessions.

In a similar way, God wants to father, or pattern, into us the inner habits that lead away from spiritual deadness and free us to engage fully in life. This is the path to health and maturity we'll explore throughout the balance of this book.

For now, as we close this chapter, I want to assure you that we are very fortunate men—because we do have a great Father who offers to restore our souls to experience freedom and strength as his sons. I'm also grateful that he has put men in my life, as he will in yours, who can be brothers, coaches, confessors, mentors, and maybe even "fathers" in faith and life. As we grow, we'll need to make wise individual choices before God; we'll also need a lot of support from other men when sticking with the right choices seems too hard.

Now that we've seen the damage that abortion has left in the lives of postabortive men and recognized their need to be redirected in some of their deepest attitudes, it's time to take some important steps toward mature manhood.

QUESTIONS

1. Early in this chapter the author asserts, "Adulthood is . . . about learning how to live with the results of your choices." Do you agree with this assertion? Why or why not?

2. Why do you think most fathers find it difficult to nurture healthy sexuality in their sons?

3. From your personal observations and experience, what is the impact of the "absent father" on young boys and girls? on adolescent and young-adult men and women? on society?

4. Do you think it is important for today's Christian man—especially a postabortive man—to have a mature Christian mentor? Why or why not?

5. Do you have such a mentor in your life? If so, describe what you appreciate about him. If not, think of three issues you would like to discuss with a mentor. Ask God to direct you to a wise, godly man who would be willing to meet regularly with you.

Four

How Do You Feel?

Rain-soaked and freezing, the two climbers were in serious trouble.

The forecast had been wrong. Now, icy blasts from the oncoming storm nearly flipped them off their ledge. At eleven thousand feet—halfway up the bare rock known as Bonatti Pillar, in the French Alps—there was no quick escape and only a deadly plunge with any misstep. The lead climber, Ruaridh Pringle, watched in horror as his younger companion, Hugo Glover, began to fumble with easy knots and mumble with the slurred speech of onset hypothermia.

Pringle had to get them both down fast. They'd been climbing two days and suffering from exhaustion when the chilling rain had suddenly lashed at them from nowhere. But to reach a safe place to descend they would still have to climb up the Pillar. Trembling with cold, Pringle was not much better off than his ailing partner, even though he had the advantage of experience.

He tried to keep Glover talking. "Tell me exactly how you feel, Hugo."

Glover's face was gray and waxy, his reply confused. He thought they were descending, and wondered why Pringle was bothering him in the middle of a tough maneuver.

Pringle felt a rush of near panic—Glover's life was in his hands. But something inside him galvanized. For hours he coaxed, pushed, and drove his buddy on. When numbness sent Glover to the ground, Pringle huddled over him, rubbing his face, torso, arms, legs—fighting to keep his friend's circulation going.

Reaching a tough vertical ascent, they saw that they were caught between layers of billowing storm clouds above and below. Lightning, a climber's worst nightmare, stung the air all around them. Glover gave up. "I can't do it," he mumbled. "Legs won't work." The look in his dismal eyes told Pringle, *Go on without me.*

"No!" Pringle shot back. "Get mad, Hugo!"

Somehow, Glover made the ascent while cannons of thunder exploded all around them. At the top of the ledge the storm was in full fury.

They'd gotten within 150 feet of the descent only to be pinned by furious winds. Pringle set up an emergency nylon shelter, and they crammed their lower bodies into sleeping bags. The raging winds whipped the nylon and spit rain into their meager shelter.

But that wasn't the worst.

Suddenly, with an ear-splitting crack, the air went white. Pringle and Glover writhed in agony as lightning struck. Once . . . twice . . . three times. Searing pain burned their legs. Pringle blacked out. He woke to his own screams and the smell of singed hair.

Weak and cold, the men could only huddle in their pathetic shelter as violent waves of storm rolled over them. Darkness descended. Over the next twelve hours, seventeen bolts of electricity would slam their bodies, each time jolting them into a wincing, fetal position.

When a murky dawn broke, Pringle forced Glover to his feet. Thunder continued to roll around them, but this was their one—last—chance. Staggering, hands and feet burning with cold, Pringle angled his friend to the path of descent. But now Pringle was past his limit. His hands had swelled and the pain was unbearable.

It was Glover's turn. "You've got to keep going," he urged. "We're gonna make it."

The words were barely out of his mouth when another electrical strike smacked them to their knees.

The descent became a tag-team match against death. Two

more lightning strikes slammed them—twenty punishing blows in all. A bridge across a glacial crevice had crumbled in the storm, forcing a half-mile detour through slush. It required every ounce of motivation, courage, and strength to keep each other going.

When Pringle and Glover staggered into a warden's chalet on the mountainside, they were changed men. They had made it through a living hell together. As they looked each other in the eye, they knew they were more than climbing buddies.

The ordeal had made them lifelong friends.[1]

Pringle and Glover are two guys who know there's at least one man in this world they can trust with their lives. And inside every one of us is a longing to know this kind of loyalty—to know that when we're at our lowest, weakest point someone will be there.

When we know we need help, we don't need someone to make us feel weak or stupid. We need a true and loyal friend, a solid guy we can talk to about our most private fears and failures. Someone who can help us over the long haul and stick with us through the toughest challenges until we get our feet on safe ground again. Someone who is a "safe place" we can go to for rest and repair—a shelter from the storm.

Like the two climbers, abortive fathers have taken some serious "lightning strikes" to the soul. But many of them have put themselves in a bind. As men, we don't like to admit our sins and mistakes—especially to other men. So we've spent a great deal of energy rationalizing, justifying, and even projecting the image that we're okay and don't need help. Where Pringle and Glover stuck together in their worst and weakest moments, we've run from ourselves and even from others—all because we don't like what we see in the mirror.

"Tell me exactly how you feel," asked Pringle. And when Glover answered honestly, his friend knew how to help. As long as we keep our pain to ourselves, we remain weak and in need. But even before we come in from the cold, some of us need to recognize exactly what our need is. It's time to ask: What am I hiding? And who am I hiding it from?

WHAT AM I HIDING?

When they're honest with themselves, abortive fathers know they hide a deep sense that they are defective, a sense that something about them is just not right.

Ricky, twice an abortive father, found himself struggling years later with an odd feeling that came over him when he talked to certain guys. These included some of the fathers of kids on his son's soccer team and even most of the guys at church. After only a few minutes of conversation, Ricky would feel he had to get out of the discussion. "When I stopped to think about it, I realized that the guys I was repelled by had the same thing in common, at least in my eyes. They were decent. When I was with them, I automatically felt like a lesser man. I couldn't take that."

The sense of defectiveness that Ricky and other abortive fathers feel is a serious consequence of abortion. It is also known by another name—shame.

Shame is the sense we live with when we feel we have not measured up to an important standard or that we've ruined something of great value. Shame is especially corrosive to the soul when the thing we've done can never be undone. It seems that our act has recorded, for all time, that we are weak, wrong, bent, flawed, marred. Shame mocks us by whispering that if others knew the truth about us, we would be rejected, shunned, and outcast.

The sense of shame many men can carry will not be erased by any kind of success. It cannot be eased even if we are showered with admiration. In fact, success and praise can make shame worse. "When I graduated with high honors from law school," says Paul, "everyone in my family was congratulating me, lavishing praise on me. I kept thinking, *You're applauding the wrong guy. I don't deserve this because I'm the rat who aborted his own baby because it was inconvenient.*" So even our success is flawed and empty because we feel we don't deserve it.

What is the root of the abortive father's shame?

In the core of his being, he has judged himself to be unworthy. When the life of his own child was devalued through abortion, he was devalued too.

Abortion interrupts a natural and crucial passage in a man's life. Participating in conceiving a child brings us to the door of manhood in a way that few other acts can. Reproducing another human being who is like us, from us, out of us, takes a man across an internal goal line, giving evidence of his masculine potency in a way nothing else can. But reproducing is more than taking part in conception because fathering involves far, far more than the macho pride that we can impregnate. It's a chance to silence the inner voices of adolescent doubt that tell us we're not responsible enough—not capable, patient, giving, sacrificing enough—to parent a child.

Abortion cripples a man because it keeps him from making that passage to maturity at a profound level. He's left knowing that somewhere back on the map of his life is a road sign that stands there like a judgment: At this turn in the road he went the wrong way.

Is it any wonder that his core identity is deeply marked? Any wonder that, out of his shame, he acts out certain unhealthy life patterns over and over again?

Many postabortive men live with the very clear sense that they will never be right again. Some turn to alcohol and drugs to medicate the pain. Others don't connect their present struggles with the past but blame other people for their problems. Chad blamed his career problems on a whole string of bosses who fired him, instead of facing up to his many irresponsible habits that tanked his productivity again and again. Some guys fight their sense of shame to the death: Jeb's first wife left him and then his second wife, both walking out with nearly identical parting lines: "I'm leaving you because you are too weak and threatened to ever admit you're at fault. You'd be okay if just once you could grow up and say, 'I'm wrong.'"

Here is the bind we find ourselves in: Only when a man has a solid sense of worth can he freely own up to his weaknesses, sins, and errors. Then and only then can he begin to learn from his errors and begin a new life. This man knows he is intrinsically worth every effort that can be made to salvage, improve, correct, and retrain him.

But a man who lives in shame has little or no such confidence. Greg keeps thinking, *I'm a murderer. I'm flawed way beyond the flaws of normal people. I'm defective in a way that can't be fixed.* And Jerry, sixteen years after the abortion that ended his first child's life, still tells himself, *I don't deserve to be happy or to be successful at my work. I don't deserve the good family I now have.*

Condemning themselves to a spiritual prison is wrong. It won't change the past. It keeps Greg and Jerry from living fully in the present and denies the future God wants for them and the people in their lives today.

Ask yourself now: Am I worth salvaging? Am I worth healing? Is it worth it to become a more mature man? If you have any doubts—and many postabortive men do—I want to assure you that in God's eyes you are indeed worth salvaging, worth healing, and worth growing into a mature man. The sin of abortion is not greater than God's payment for your life when he sent his Son to die on the cross.

Beginning to heal the hidden shame that plagues us requires a look at ourselves as we are right now. And it requires us to ask some probing questions.

WHAT ARE WE HIDING FROM?

As "fugitives," many abortive fathers run, literally or figuratively, from certain situations that might expose their flaws. More importantly, they tend to run from certain types of people. We touched on this in an earlier chapter, but now we need to pause and look at why men run.

Shame is painful, exposing us at our worst. We turn our faces and avoid eye contact, keeping the eyes of others from looking into our soul where they might see the small, miserable creature standing there looking worthy of rejection.

In this isolation, we're no different from our father, Adam, who imagined he could hide in the bushes and avoid even the eyes of God (see Genesis 3). Ironically, shame makes us run from sources of help because we see that what we've done cannot be changed—and so we believe we are no longer worthy of help. Many abortive men spend years running from God. Sure, they may be in church. They may be involved in community and human services. But often that involvement is an attempt to offer some payment for their sin—even though they know the offering is far from adequate. By trying to correct the past rather than build a future, too many men become paralyzed in the aftermath of abortion.

At the same time, many men spend years cutting themselves off from a whole range of relationships that could help heal their shame. They cut themselves off mainly because something about the relationship makes them feel uncomfortable—though they may not even know what that something is.

What follows is a small catalog of the kinds of people you may be avoiding because being with them makes you feel somewhat uncomfortable. I'd like you to read this section carefully and honestly assess the kinds of people you may habitually avoid or move away from.

- *"Good" people.* Some people are pictures of innocence and niceness. Sure, we know they're human, too—yet something about them just says *goodness.* In this category we may include pastors, strong and spiritual men, family men, and guys who generally seem to be uncomplicated and at peace.

Men who carry shame can find themselves driven away from people like this. They say, "They're *too* nice. Maybe too good to be true." What they mean is, "It makes me uncomfortable to be around someone who is such a strong reminder that I am not that good."

- *"Dangerous" people.* By *dangerous* I mean the kind of people who seem to be able to see right through us. Whether they are gentle or bold and outspoken, we don't like the sense that they can look past our image and see inside. Dangerous people are those who want to move in close and talk at deeper personal levels.

Many men recognize that they retreat from good people but do not recognize that they put others in the dangerous category. Tom had huge fights with his wife when she claimed that he had trashed numerous friendships, driving away a number of really good guys who wanted to be his buddy. One day, he got into it with her in front of a guy he'd known through a hunting club. Turning to Peter for support, Tom asked, "Do I push away friends when they get too close?" Without missing a beat, Peter replied, "Yes, you do. You've done it to me."

Men who carry shame say, "I'm a private kind of guy, that's all." What they mean is, "I'm uncomfortable around someone who might get a look at how sick and terrible I am."

- *"Incapable" people.* Somewhere in the back of our minds we know we live with heavy issues that are not easily resolved. They could shock people if they came to light. People we judge to be incapable of offering help or advice, or incapable of dealing with our secrets, get crossed off the guest list of possible friends.

Men who carry shame say, "They can't help anyway, so why do they need to know?" Or "They can't handle what I tell them without flipping out. Who needs that?" What these men mean is, *I think my sin or flaw is so bad that I can never be right.*

Postabortive fathers need to realize that other people do not make them uncomfortable. Rather, they are uncomfortable living with themselves, and other people only trigger the discomfort that's already present in their lives.

Condemning themselves feels like the right thing to do. After all, they committed a terrible act, right? But self-condemnation easily becomes self-punishment. And abortive fathers punish themselves endlessly, telling themselves they are no good and deserve no mercy because they showed no mercy to their own offspring.

This self-deprecation manifests itself in the presence of people who, even in a small way, reflect the glory of God. When postabortive men find themselves in "good" company, they feel compelled to run. They run because the look of mercy and kindness—which they're convinced they don't deserve—is too painful to bear. Judging themselves harshly, they would rather face punishment and pain than bear God's forgiveness.

They have lived with the consequences. It's time to stop and face the mercy.

GETTING YOUR STRENGTH BACK

The real problem with self-condemnation is that it's often based on some measure of truth.

Many abortive men feel deeply ashamed because they carry a painful secret about themselves. As males, they like to be strong, powerful, and in control. When they're honest, though, they know that the act of sacrificing the life of a child was unmasculine and weak. Their choice has left them feeling defective.

Many of you allowed peers or girlfriends to have power over you by giving in to their pressure to have sex before you were ready to handle the consequences. A lot of guys say, "I wouldn't have done it if my buddies didn't give me such a hard time about being a virgin." Or "I was afraid the other guys wouldn't think I was normal." Or "She wanted me to prove I loved her."

What causes men to give their power away? Fear. They believed the opinion and acceptance of others were so important that they feared living without it. More than one guy has given up his masculine power to the fear that he might not be manly enough or desirable enough. Or to the fear that he might be gay. Believe it or not, some guys give in to the fear that they are "too religious." Not wanting to look like religious weirdos, they set out to prove they can be just as carnal as the next guy. There is also the basic, consumerist kind of fear that overtakes certain guys. It's the fear that says (at the risk of sounding base), "I just want to get some."

Acting out of fear, rather than solid conviction, always weakens a man.

If you are a postabortive man, these are the voices that you listened to, and now you know this was a huge mistake. You weren't beasts who needed to prove your siring abilities. You were more than gross consumers. You should never have made choices to be accepted by other people. Not one of them had a vested interest in the outcome of your choices. Friends, girlfriends, and even our culture influenced you, then left you to bear the consequences of your choices alone.

It's important to get a handle on the people and the voices that influence us. If we don't recognize their power, they will continue to lead us by the nose. But there is one person we need to face right now—a person who may be fighting really hard to keep out of sight.

WHO ARE WE *REALLY* AFRAID TO FACE?
Sometimes the person we are most afraid to face is our true self—who we are at the core of our being.

When you stand at the mirror shaving, who is the man staring back at you? Can you even look him in the eye?

I believe the look in the eye of an abortive man is a look that accuses. *You are inadequate,* it says. Inadequacy is a potent force that will influence you more than anything else—today and every day for the rest of your life unless something deep within you is radically transformed.

What does that sense of inadequacy look like?

Men have always wanted to belong among other men. For all of our solitary impulses—and most men have them—we carry an almost tribal instinct that makes us want to be among fathers, uncles, brothers, and male friends, proving that we belong among other masculine creatures. At the same time, we also want to be desirable to women, to prove we're acceptable as sexual partners. Along with that, we want to be protectors and trainers of our children, proving that we are capable of self-giving. And at the deepest level, we want permanent acceptance. Why? Because knowing we're accepted—no matter who or what we are, no matter what we do—makes us feel valued.

That's the big problem, though, isn't it? We're convinced that if other people could view our secret lives, they'd recoil in shock.

FACING GOD

All our running and hiding have kept us from facing other people, and even ourselves. It's also kept us from facing God. We sense that we're flawed—marked men in every sense of the word. If God got ahold of us, what would he do?

At the root of it all, we have a more deeply spiritual problem than we knew. Will we ever be safe and rest easy again? Many abortive men live with constant wariness, like a shadow on the back wall of their soul, that God is about to do something terrible to them as payback for what they've done.

Kendall and his wife have been unable to conceive a child. "I know," he confides, "that I'm the problem. God is punishing me with infertility."

Nick faithfully attends church and tries to serve God. Even so, he believes his job failures and several broken relationships with Christian women are signs of God's rejection.

Jim lives under a cloud. He believes he's required to pay God back his whole life by living a very strict and even legalistic existence.

Many abortive men live with constant wariness, like a shadow on the back wall of their soul, that God is about to do something terrible to them as payback for what they've done.

Our core identity—the way we see ourselves—is what drives us to do what we do. One guy sees himself as competent and handsome, and he goes out and knocks the world to its knees. Another guy with the same competence and looks sees himself as a reject, and he can't even look the world in the eye.

Abortive men have taken on the identity of marked men. So it's little wonder that they run and little wonder that they struggle with the stamp of unworthiness. Yes, by listening to the wrong voices, they made some very bad choices. Mercilessly they condemn themselves. Perhaps that's why, in their own mind's eye, they believe they see the condemning face of God; they feel his anger and the way his fists must be clenched, waiting to strike.

They have taken their own anger and desire to punish themselves and have imagined that these are God's reactions to them now. And so they live ill at ease, ready to run for shelter from the oncoming storm, just waiting for lightning to strike.

Like the young climber at the beginning of this chapter, they need someone who will never leave or abandon them in their worst need. Someone who will remain loyal and lead them out of the jam they're in—even when they want to give up to the forces that want to crush them.

That someone is God—not the angry God they've imagined, but the Father of mercy and grace who seeks and heals his lost, hurting sons.

FACING YOURSELF AS GOD SEES YOU

In the New Testament, God tells us that he is the keeper of the true identity of every man. He promises that those who overcome every impulse to run and hide from him—that is, those who simply *come* to him—will be given the gift of a "new name," the identity God himself gives us signifies the way he sees us (see Revelation 2:17).

Our core identity is a gift from God who made us. And so he is the One we need to face—openly, honestly, out from behind our mask of shame. In our heart of hearts, we are on a quest to be blessed by him.

Instead of running from God, it's time we learn how to trust him so he can remake our core identity as he sees us. How do we do that? First, we can allow him to lead us back to the place where we made the wrong choice, took the wrong path, and turned aside from the passage to true manhood. We can also

begin to let his voice replace all the other voices we've ever listened to, including our own voice of self-condemnation.

Take some time right now to search your soul and listen
carefully to the voices that speak to you. Do they condemn
you? mock you? tell you that you have no right to serve God
or pretend you're a decent man? You must learn to stop
agreeing with voices that do not speak with the grace and
mercy of God. Picture yourself from God's viewpoint—small,
flawed, sinful—and hear his voice speak the word he wants you
to hear: *Forgiven.*

Now listen carefully to the old judgments that have weighed
you down. Do voices insist you're a fraud? Worthless? A sick or
evil man? Danny recalls, "When I got quiet and really listened,
I was shocked. I'd been a Christian for years after the abortion.
But deep inside, a cold voice would whisper to me, *You're damned
to hell for what you did.* I had to turn to God to hear his verdict
instead."

START AGREEING WITH GOD

We must begin to agree with God's assessment of us and our
lives. Of course, the starting point is to agree with God that it
was wrong to sire and abandon a child to death by abortion.
Many of us have already been beating ourselves up emotionally
about this. But when we agree with God, there is a major difference: God sees all sins alike. He is as quick to show mercy to
the man who asks forgiveness for lying as he is to the man who
seeks forgiveness for abortion. We're talking about "a forgiving
God, . . . slow to anger and abounding in love" (Nehemiah
9:17).

We must also agree with God that the sacrifice of his Son,
Jesus Christ, is the act of atonement for our sins. We are worthy of forgiveness because Jesus paid a price for our sin that
we could not pay. Many abortive fathers have been trying
really hard to be "good men"—serving in the church or community, being generous with friends, giving to other families,
coaching kids—all in an effort to make up for what they did.
They hope God will see their efforts and maybe tip the scales

> **God sees all sins alike. He is as quick to show mercy to the man who asks forgiveness for lying as he is to the man who seeks forgiveness for abortion.**

of justice in their favor. Good as it is to give of ourselves, we can never buy God's favor. The New Testament tells us God's forgiveness and grace are free gifts, as is the blood of Christ that was given to save us eternally (Ephesians 1:7 and 2:8). We must agree with God that his saving work is perfect and stop trying to earn our way with him.

Finally, they need to agree with God that they *can* be transformed and experience a whole new identity. Instead of living as marked men, they can become sons of the heavenly Father—solid men who can lead and be relied upon, good friends, good husbands, and good fathers—men who can walk with vision in their eyes and a spring in their steps as they pursue that vision.

These are the profound changes you can experience in your life—if you are willing to continue the "consequential journey" you have embarked upon.

BEFORE IT GETS BETTER

As we go deeper into the life God has for you, it's likely that you will experience remorse, regret, and other kinds of emotional pain. The more open and honest you become, the more shame you may experience—but be assured it is only temporary. Healing is always the same—whether you undergo knee surgery after a biking accident or experience emotional and spiritual healing: It usually feels worse before it gets better. Yet the rewards of health, inner freedom, and new masculine strength are going to be well worth any pain you may feel getting there.

And so, as we move ahead in our next chapter, your goal is to stand honestly, openly before God, allowing him to do the painful, deep, transforming work that you need.

QUESTIONS

1. What do you think made Pringle and Glover go on and not give up? What does their story illustrate about the nature and value of a true, loyal friend? What other lesson(s) did you learn from their story that you can use in your journey to wholeness?
2. What is your level of comfort around other guys—especially those you look up to? What is the source of any discomfort you might feel?
3. Do you feel comfortable in church? in worship? in a group of men who are being honest about their struggles, emotions, or spiritual growth? Explain why or why not.
4. Before you read this chapter, what did you believe God thinks of you? Now that you've read it, how has that perception changed?

Five

Maker of Our Soul

If any of you are *Star Trek* viewers, you may have caught this movie-length episode:

The Voyager satellite, orbiting in the endless night of space, is damaged and gets thrown off course. Fitted with its own high-tech systems for self-repair, it tries to right itself . . . and through some fluke it begins to amass power and intelligence along with a dark side. Suddenly this benign satellite becomes destructive. It develops a pathological life of its own.

Unfortunately, as the malignant impulses gain force, the satellite zeros in on the good spaceship Enterprise as a target for destruction. Only fast thinking by the crew saves them from death. However, the satellite has been programmed to know that when a major glitch occurs it's time to seek out its maker.

The writers of this episode touched on an important and universal theme, one that every man can recognize: When we have a serious problem, something in us automatically seeks a way back to our Maker. Unfortunately, there's also a defect in us—a frustrated, angry, destructive energy—that can keep us from receiving help from the only One who can save us from ourselves.

It's time to dismantle the frustration and resistance and meet with the Maker of our soul.

FACE-TO-FACE

One source of a man's frustration, resistance, and shame can be his sexuality. Many guys think, *There must be something wrong with me, to feel so driven by sex so much of the time.* Or, *Maybe there's something wrong with my thoughts and the things I desire.*

But God is the One who created your masculine identity, the One who gave you the body chemistry that constitutes the intensity of the male urge. And not only did he create us this way, he did so for a purpose.

When God created the first man, Adam, he gave him an amazing ability. Within Adam's body, chemicals came together that charged him with an incredible potency: the power to beget other human life. God approved this power of physical procreation, saying, "Be fruitful and increase . . ." (see Genesis 1 and 2), giving his blessing to our intense drive for sexual connection.

Just as important, God created within our soul another potent force—the ability to form intimate spiritual connections and to "become one" with another person. This kind of oneness describes the melding together of two personalities that comes about through loyalty, commitment, and deep understanding of one another. It's this longing to become united in spirit with another person that we see in Adam when, searching among all the creatures God has created, he's disappointed because he can't find anyone like him to connect with (Genesis 2:20). It's this longing that we hear throughout the Psalms as the soul of man desires to connect deeply with God.

And yet men tend to resist this deeper connection. We're like the satellite that knows it needs to seek its source, but to surrender all that's in us to someone else—and the helpless, weak feeling that it brings—is something most of us hate. Why?

To be connected to someone—to God, to a woman—means that we must become known intimately, for exactly who we are. It means bringing to light all of our needs and wants—what angers and disgusts us as well as the things that really please us. It means bringing all of who we are out into the light for another to see.

Is it any wonder most of us have been running?

"The Lord looks at the heart" (1 Samuel 16:7). And nothing is hidden from him (Hebrews 4:13).

At the base of it all, our flight from manhood is a flight from the all-seeing eyes of God. Since he has the ultimate power, many of us live with a buried fear of facing him. But showing God our back as we run only delays the face-off. The psalmist wrote, "Where can I go from your Spirit? . . . [Wherever I go] you are there" (Psalm 139:7-8). Just when we think we've left God in the dust, we'll turn a corner and find him already there waiting for us.

If you were to face God right now, what look would you see in his eyes?

Some abortive fathers fake indifference—but it's a cover-up. Some grovel before God, telling themselves what worms they are—all the while hating the unmanly way they feel. Some who become Christians get legalistic. Or they become activists, making an idol of the cause. All may be trying to earn an atonement they feel they don't deserve.

These are unsatisfying ways for any man to live because he may never feel that he's standing on solid ground. Earlier we talked about this in a different way, referring to the instability many postabortive men feel—the sense of being a chameleon and changing to fit the company they're in.

A major source of spiritual instability in every man is knowing we live in God's universe, yet not knowing how he really feels toward us. Some of us may even say we know we're forgiven when we really believe he's angry or disgusted with us or that we'll always be tainted in his eyes.

The healing of our masculine soul will come only as we learn to reconnect with God. Only he, who made our soul, is capable of restoring it and setting us on the path of healthy maturity again.

This means learning to be open and honest before God and then learning how to receive his help. But taking this first step of total openness and honesty can be the most difficult because postabortive men often don't feel safe enough to be vulnerable

The healing of our masculine soul will come only as we learn to reconnect with God.

before God. The abortion in your past may cause you to fear retribution. Yet God loves you (1 John 4:9-10), and he will heal you as you learn how to be open and trusting before him. But only total honesty will help you begin reclaiming the ground of responsible adulthood you forfeited.

I promise you that if you can get through just this first step, you are on your way home. Make the effort, and you will find yourself on the way to a fully restored manhood!

FACING YOUR LOSSES
God wants to help us face what has been lost to us through our past actions. Painful as it may be, it's time to own up to them and ask God to forgive and heal us.

We Have Lost Years of Healthy Growth toward Adulthood
Deep down, every one of us knows we were created to be life givers, not life takers. To make little copies of ourselves—not just physically but spiritually. That's because we instinctively want to preserve our lineage.

But as we have already seen, we aborted our own maturity when we participated in aborting a child. Even if we have gone on to rear other children, a big piece of our lives is still missing. There is a part of our past that is painful and that we don't like to share. Quite likely we feel we've lost the right to speak on moral issues or to offer advice to others: *Who am I to talk? What makes me think I have anything to say to help some-one else?*

We Have Lost a Piece of Our Privacy
Since it is the most intimate act between two people, the act of sex reveals a lot about us. When guys who have had one or more sexual partners go on to marry someone else, there can be a lasting, discomfiting sense that someone else out there knows what they look like, act like, and sound like during the sex act.

And if that premarital sex resulted in pregnancy and abortion, at least one other person on earth knows that they participated in the unhappy act of ending a child's life.

The net effect is that an important piece of our privacy is lost for good.

We Have Lost a Piece of Our Hearts

Years later . . . decades later . . . men who have not found healing from the abortion experience still feel painful heart-bonds to the child they lost. Many feel a faint emotional/spiritual connection to the woman who was their partner at the time—even if they've both gone on and married other people.

Beyond these broken heart-bonds, some men suffer a sense of loss for another reason: They may have made promises or commitments to the women they were sleeping with. When they said "I love you—I want to marry you" or "I'll always be there for you, no matter what," they may have meant it, but circumstances changed radically, and they went back on their word.

So they're left with a painful sense of loss and a nagging question: *What is my word worth now?* The part of their hearts that once had integrity now seems empty.

We May Have Lost the Motivation to Be Successful

Raymond recalls, "I'd been on a good career track. I was a leader in my church. But after the abortion I sort of knocked around for years from one dead-end job to another. I dropped back on everything. My self-esteem, my sense of worth, sort of zeroed out. I didn't care what happened to me. So I lost my desire to do anything but put a little money in my pocket to pay the bills. As far as growing in a career—I couldn't have cared less."

When a man becomes a father, several positive motivations emerge naturally inside him. Among these is the motivation to better himself, which in turn makes him more valuable to employers and therefore capable of being a better provider for his new child. A side benefit is that as he grows in skills and work achievements, he feels better about himself because he is living up to his potential.

Another motivation that emerges with new fathers is the desire to provide a good life for their child. Of course, we each have different standards of what we mean by "a good life," but the point is that conceiving, birthing, and raising a child provide special incentive to a father. A side benefit is that he also learns to move away from self-centeredness and begins to focus more on the needs of others—a very healthy step toward masculine maturity.

But for too many men, abortion stifled these motivations.

We Have Lost Our Connection with the Man We Wanted to Be

Why is it that so many guys connect with movie heroes such as Indiana Jones, the adventure hero, or Jack Dawson, the hero from *Titanic?* In large part it's because we feel drawn to be like them—not petty and self-centered but morally stronger and physically tougher than we know ourselves to be.

Indiana Jones is a Renaissance kind of guy, a professor who is as much at home in a university classroom as he is inside temple ruins in a steaming jungle. Sure, he can deliver a mean punch, but he's kind to women—even a bit old-fashioned and bashful. And he can't help risking his life if it means saving a child. As much as men are drawn to the edge-of-your-seat action of the stories, we like "Indy" because he overcomes evil with virtue.

Jack Dawson is another guy millions of us connect with. He's carefree but not irresponsible. When he meets a young woman—Rose—who is desperate and about to take her own life, he doesn't back off or pretend it's none of his business. He promises to stick with her even if she jumps into the icy Atlantic. "I'm involved now," he asserts. And in the end, he selflessly gives his life to save Rose.

We also connect with guys like Olympic speed skater Dan Jansen. After several heartbreaking losses in earlier Olympics, he pushed himself hard to finally take the gold medal. He shared his moment of glory with his young daughter, holding her in his arms as he skated the victory lap.

What we admire in other men—heroism, humility, bravery, old-fashioned modesty in a brazen world, and selflessness—we would like to see in ourselves. Every one of us starts out with the hope that we have the potential for greatness. Those who participated in abortion, however, live with a deep grief—a sadness caused by the sense that they have lost that potential forever and can never become the men they would like to be.

We Have Lost a Child and Something Else Besides

"Every year on the anniversary of the abortion I experience a terrible pain inside—thinking about the life that was lost," says Ricardo. "The home runs that will never be hit. Or the dance recitals that will never be. The contribution to this world that's lost—maybe in medicine or some other human service. It's an ache in me."

Inside the heart of every abortive father is a deep sense of grief because he knows he gave up a relationship with a unique person who was part of him.

That in itself is an ache only God can heal. Yes, there is grief for the literal child who was lost. But along with that there is an ache that comes from our unnameable loss.

Abortive men often lose the ability to envision themselves as better men. We made a choice that cut us off from the God-given power to become manly in every aspect of our being.

To face God the Creator is to discover that we are not growing as he intended. Instead, we're stuck. We're left with a static self, experiencing little emotional or spiritual growth. We're left in a torn state as men who feel condemned within but who live out on the surface of life, pretending that we're really good guys so others will like us.

We deeply, desperately need to reconnect with God. Only he can restore—or help us see for the first time—the vision of what we can become as forgiven, healthy men.

HOW GOD SEES YOU

The wonderful thing about God's vision for a man is that it's not one of the clichéd images the world tosses at us. Most of us are weary of trying to live up to false images of masculinity and manhood. We see through the shallow images of successful man, tough guy, rogue, good ol' boy, and playboy—even the pious perfect man.

The image that God wants to create in us has far more to do
with inner qualities. Just as God's true nature is made known
by his character, so it can be for us if we allow him to help us
grow as his spiritual sons.

Though you may not sense any of these inner qualities at
the moment, I can assure you that the way God still sees you
as a man includes the following traits:

1. You Are an Initiator
You may see yourself right now as a passive follower. But God
does not see you as a nobody who slouches along the sidelines
of life, allowing circumstances to drag you along. God sees
you as a man who can take responsibility for making choices,
great and small—not only for yourself, but for others, too. He
regards you as a man who can bring godly direction back to
your life.

2. You Are a Protector
You are not created just to be a "daddy bear," a guy who keeps
physical danger and evil away from those you love. You are
created by God to be a man who knows how to protect his own
spirit from the corroding forces of decadence and evil and to
protect the spirits of others in your charge.

3. You Have Authority
No, you have not given up standing for what's good or standing
against what's destructive and evil. God created us to be moral
beings who can use moral judgment wisely to protect and
advance what's good. We don't need to tell the world, or any
other person, how we know so well that wrong is wrong; we
need only to speak with the authority that painful personal
experience has given us.

4. You Are Compassionate with Weakness and Failure
Who more than an abortive man knows what it's like to make a
terrible choice? Or to experience devastating loss caused by
human selfishness or blindness? Or to suffer?

The proud, self-righteous man can offer little help to a lost, hurting world. But God sees you as one who can offer compassion, understanding, and help to others because you know the destructiveness of your past weakness and failure.

5. You Are Teachable . . . and a Teacher of Others

God sees you as men who can accept constructive criticism and direction without being threatened. Because you've been brought to your knees in humility, you are more open to being taught about life and how to live it. New possibilities are open to you.

6. You Are Loving . . . and Lovable

When God looks at you, he sees a son he greatly loves. He also sees that you have the potential to be healed of a frozen heart—to allow love, kindness, patience, generosity, and goodness to flow through you to others as never before.

THE BIRTH OF RESTORATION

When we're on the run from our God-given identity, we live in subjection to our feelings. Many men bristle at this suggestion because we like to think that only women give in to emotions such as hurt, fear, or sadness. But we really know better. We know we're sometimes subject to wide mood swings—on top of the world in the morning and in the pits by afternoon. Maybe we can identify what triggers our mood swings and maybe we can't. Without our God-given identity we're also easily affected by put-downs, insults, and slights. We can be touchy, reactive to even small, well-intended criticisms. And when events go against us, we can feel thoroughly trashed by life.

But when we move toward the solid character God wants to restore in us, it's as if we've left the shifting sand and gained secure footing on solid ground. We're subject only to what God's Word says about us—not to the opinions of others, or to circumstances, or even to our own changing feelings. Moreover, we become more subject to God's guidance and direction so we learn to listen, even through the correction of others, for God's voice redirecting us. Our sin has less and less hold over our self-image and opinions of ourselves.

When we submit to God's fatherhood over us, we open the floodgate of restoration. This, and nothing less, is what the Maker of our souls had in mind when he fashioned us and designed a purpose for our lives.

No doubt you've caught glimpses of yourself throughout this chapter. Perhaps you've realized for the first time the terrible losses abortion has brought to your life. Or maybe you've finally been able to acknowledge the weaknesses that make life a struggle and compared them to the wonderful, positive character traits of the man you would like to become.

> **When we submit to God's fatherhood, we open the floodgate of restoration.**

Now is the time to face God with your pain and need and renewed hopes. He is present with you, though you cannot see or feel him. And he is calling you to himself, wanting to meet face-to-face with you, forgive you, and embrace you.

As we close this chapter, I suggest that you make a step toward God that you may not have made before. Speak to him openly and honestly about your regrets, your desire for forgiveness, and your desire to be delivered from the shame that has made you feel disqualified for Christian manhood. In humble prayer, let him help you uncover, acknowledge, and shoulder the truth. He alone can help you bear the weight and pain of what was truly lost, just as he alone can restore your vision of the man you can still become by his grace and power.

In a moment of quiet, go to him now. The Father of love and mercy is waiting for you.

QUESTIONS

1. If you were face-to-face with God right now, what look would you see in his eyes? Why do you believe this?
2. How do the losses brought about by the abortion experience affect the way you view God? the way you view yourself?

3. Review the character traits listed in the section titled "How God Sees You." How does it make you feel to know that God sees this kind of potential in you?
4. Is there any good reason why you cannot or should not take the step of prayer suggested at the end of the chapter? Why not take five or ten minutes right now and meet face-to-face with God? (He's looking forward to it. So can you.)

Six

Rescued from the Enemy

We live with the illusion that we are free men—empowered to choose what we want.

Western culture fosters that illusion by harping about individual rights and personal fulfillment. Inner voices foster the illusion too, telling us to resist anything that might keep us from seeking any fulfillment or fantasy we desire. Limitation—or control—is seen as the great evil.

However . . .

God's way of growing us into men of character and quality is to give us training and discipline for our souls. The fact that personal growth and training go hand in hand is a lifelong principle.

Tim wants to make it in business, so he seeks training by learning all the disciplines that will lead him to an MBA.

Roy has a dream of getting into the Special Forces, so he submits himself to the rigorous training that puts him ahead of the average military grunt.

In so many spheres of life we accept training—its limitations and hard work—because we have a vision of the goal beyond the struggle. Without even thinking about it, we embrace such virtues as personal discipline and delayed gratification. But when you chose abortion—just as when you choose any other sin—you pulled away from the spiritual training of manhood your soul needs.

In the previous chapter we began meeting face-to-face with God, the Maker of our souls, the One who knows how to train the masculine spirit to be healthy and mature. We began our consequential journey with him, counting the cost of what was lost to us when we chose to go another way. Tough as it is, only his training can make us strong in spirit now. If we skip his disciplines, we only continue to weaken ourselves. Not only that, we leave ourselves in great danger, vulnerable to our soul's great enemy who, as the Bible puts it, prowls the earth like a lion looking for whomever he can devour (see 1 Peter 5:8).

THE LURE OF THE FALSE GODS

The second step we need to take with God is to face the things that now overpower us in our immaturity and weakness—that is, the false gods that lure and entrap us. What do I mean by a "false god"?

A false god is any power you rely on other than God himself in the belief that it can help you get what you want. False gods tempt us to seek happiness by walking away from the true God—and away from his plan for fulfilling our masculine identity.

> **A false god is any power you rely on other than God himself in the belief that it can help you get what you want.**

And so a false god takes the place of the true God—literally, in our inmost being—mesmerizing us with dream images we serve. False gods direct us with subtle and powerful voices that speak just at the edge of our conscious mind, *If you do this, I can give you what you want.*

What are some of the false gods we turn to, and how do they fail us? Here are just three examples.

The Image of Success

Brent was always lured by the image of success—but following the abortion, his ambitions kicked into overdrive. He'd encouraged Leslie to get the abortion so that a baby wouldn't hold him back from becoming the man of his dreams, the guy with the best suits, the best cars, and the money to pursue his expensive hobbies such as big-game hunting. But over the years, success has begun to fail him, leaving him empty. Years ago Brent lost the rush he once felt when other people complimented or admired his accomplishments. Now he feels trapped in his empty pursuit of the next big business deal and his next hunting trek.

Personal Freedom

Wilton gets angry with his wife when she begs him to stop procrastinating and organize his business records. "My produce distributorship makes us a lot of money. So my files are a mess. So I owe some back taxes. So I skimmed some money from the business to buy a boat. I'm not perfect—okay? I never claimed to be. If everybody would just get off my case, I'd work things out my way, in my own time." What he's protecting is the false god of personal freedom (also known as "the right to be irresponsible")—an immature and weak way of ignoring the requirements of responsible adult living. But the truth is that after years of this behavior, Wilton feels pretty adolescent and stupid much of the time.

Peace at Any Price

Jarell infuriates his boss, his wife, and his friends by making a joke out of the most serious issues. "I crack jokes because everyone else needs to chill out. Everyone takes things way too seriously." But the truth is that conflict makes Jarell so deeply uncomfortable that he spends his life in service to the false god of "peace at any price." To Jarell, a false peace is worth more than the strength that comes as we work to resolve real conflicts. But the inner stress he carries all the time is ruining his health, and he knows it.

These are just a few examples of the many things that can become false gods in our lives. Not just tangible items like luxury cars, dream homes, or fat bank accounts but intangible things such as escape, lust, personal vanity, or control in relationships. Even spiritual-looking pursuits can become false gods: After ending two children's lives through abortion, Stew-

art experienced a spiritual conversion and threw himself into
Christian service, hoping that serving God would have the
power to erase his sense of guilt and shame.

The problem with false gods is that they need continual
offerings from us. Their power doesn't last, and the shallow
relief they bring from fear, stress, or guilt is short-lived. Only
by living in an intimate, ever-deepening, daily relationship
with the true God can we find the forgiveness, peace, and real
freedom we need to become stable, healthy men. Just as false
gods take, condemn, and consume, the real God gives, cor-
rects, and restores.

That's why we must honestly identify the false gods we rely
on, renounce their claim on us, and agree with God that these
idols are weakening our inner man. We must agree with God
that continuing to seek fulfillment from false gods is a sin
against both him and ourselves.

How do we take this step? God has already shown us in his
Word how fugitives like us can come home.

WHEN FALSE GODS FAIL

"There was a man who had two sons. . . ." So begins one of
Jesus' most moving parables—the story of the Prodigal Son.

As the story begins, the youngest of two sons complains
to his father that he's tired of working on his father's estate.
In the distance, at night, he can see the bright lights of the
big city, and the sight makes his heart race. His head fills up
with "big man" fantasies . . . of lavishing friends with booze
and women . . . and being envied by every guy he knows.
Here, he feels like a kid. There, he'd be top man. With these
thoughts ringing in his head, he gets angry. His father's been
gypping him, making him work like a slave when he could be
partying!

"Give me my inheritance now, old man," he tells his sad-
eyed father, "and I'm out of here."

When he hits town, the hip crowd is wowed. The car, the
clothes, the haircut, the luxury apartment—he's got it all. He
is the party machine, and the crowd follows wherever he goes.

But one day the bills come due and the flow of mind-altering substances slows down. Half the crowd leaves. Some weeks later the bank takes the car, and the landlord boots him out. Only two friends are left—because they're too drunk to walk home. The young man lies down on a curb only to have two guys with Saturday night specials rob him of his wallet and expensive watch. He hocks his Italian suit and shoes and begs some worn threads from Goodwill. All alone now, he haunts the alleys behind fast-food joints, eating out of Dumpsters. Some of his old friends drive by one day, and mistaking him for any other bum on the street, try to nail him with an empty beer can—shouting, "Loser!"

The party is over. The image he created of himself is shattered. His false gods lie in ruin beside him in the gutter.

You know the end of the story. The young man comes to his senses, faces the chasm of emptiness he feels inside, and heads home—deeply humbled and hoping to work for his father as a hired hand.

But there is an important spiritual element to this story we cannot overlook.

In part, the parable tells us that everything that lures us away from God will run its course, leaving us alone and hungry again—probably even hungrier than before. The guy who indulges his desire for irresponsible sex by using pornography will always find that the thrill wears off. The magazines and videos that gave him a rush yesterday have to be replaced today. Not only that, but the images need to be wilder and kinkier than before to give him the same thrill.

In the end, no matter what our false god is, every one of us who pursues gods other than God will come up empty. And we are likely to experience the embittered spirit that comes with self-indulgence. Guys who hit this dead emptiness of the soul wind up telling themselves, *Life is just a pigsty. Everything is empty.*

Have you experienced times of emptiness? A hollow bitterness toward life? What have you been trying to fill your life with? How well have these false gods really served you?

With God's help, you need to judge the false gods for what they are.

The thing about false gods and dream images of ourselves is that they do not die easily. And so it's time to ask God for help in answering an urgent question: Are the temptations that caused me to choose abortion still in power—in any measure at all—in my life?

Jesus never tells us that the Prodigal Son participated in abortion. But without violating the Bible, I'd say there was a good chance he could have fathered an illegitimate child—a kid who would have wound up scrounging for food in the streets along with his outcast mother. Or the child would have been left in the wilderness to die. In any case, the young man was tempted by fun and irresponsibility and the chance to be a big man, but the voices that lured him drained the power from him. The same dynamic happens in us. The forces we embrace only sap us of our vitality.

Art talked his new wife into an abortion because a child would interfere with his medical school plans and her law school degree. To this day, they base their lives on the belief that success, money, and professional image are all-important—that these things will get them the happiness, fulfillment, and sense of personal importance they want. To Art, relationships tend to be shallow and secondary. Serving on a church board or helping with a charitable function keeps him from dealing with deeper spiritual issues.

Sam sort of drifted into an abortion. His girlfriend was undecided, and his attitude—as usual—was "whatever." He "allowed" the abortion, which is another way to say he passively chose it. Why? Because to this day Sam worships the false god of life without commitments, a vision of a carefree life in which no one at all relies on him. As a result, he went through a few live-in relationships before letting a woman talk him into marriage. It didn't last. Neither did the second go-round. Along the way he did father two kids, but he feels like a shabby dad to them. He rarely keeps his word. And since he hates feeling that he has disappointed someone—

especially his kids—he always hedges his promises with "maybe" and "if I can" and "if something doesn't come up." Mostly he keeps his distance and justifies it by saying, "It's better for them if I stay out of their lives." Sadly, Sam lives with a sense that he's done nothing of lasting value and that he's left a trail of sad, disappointed people in his path.

And so the destructive work of the false gods goes on and on . . . unless we turn to the God whose restoring power stops their forces.

LYING VOICES

The Prodigal Son brushed the dirt from his crummy jeans and headed for the highway to hitchhike home. Despite his shame and embarrassment, he knew he needed his father. I don't doubt that a voice in his head kept calling him back: *Stay here. You can be "the man" again!*

Whenever we try to turn from our old ways and return to our Father, voices inside will call us back. Are you still serving old voices that keep telling you:

- "Choose your own path. Only you know what's best for you."
- "Serving other people instead of serving just yourself makes you weak. When you give, you lose. It's stupid."
- "You should never let a woman or anyone else have the upper hand. You need to be in control at all times."
- "Life was made for fun. Stop taking this responsibility stuff—and this spiritual stuff—so seriously. It's not cool."

There is a real choice to be made when we're down: The Prodigal Son could have chosen to listen to the voices of lesser gods and to continue his desperate subsistence; fortunately for him and his loved ones, he chose instead to humble himself and return to the loving arms of his father.

Likewise, if we are still listening to lesser voices and obeying false gods, we're leaving ourselves wide open to the

The Prodigal Son could have chosen to continue his desperate subsistence; fortunately for him and his loved ones, he chose instead to humble himself and return to the loving arms of his father.

possibility of betraying our spouses, our children, ourselves, and ultimately, our Father—the true God. We're left in our fugitive subsistence, running from the chance to become the men God wants us to become. On the other hand, if we want to escape the destruction of our relationships and our masculine soul—both past and future destruction—we need to recognize and renounce the gods that have power over us. We need to recognize their subtle voices as they influence our thoughts and behavior. In this way, we can shake their dirt from our clothes and freely return to the company of the Father.

To help you assess the power of false gods in your life, you may find it helpful to take some time alone in a place where you can record your thoughts honestly. Take paper and pen and carefully, openly, complete these statements:

- "It's important to me to see myself as _____."
  (You might finish that statement by writing: "admired by beautiful women" or "successful and admired by other men." The important thing is to be perfectly honest with yourself before God.)
- "If I get what I want, I will become _____."
  ("acceptable," "strong and confident")
- "If I do not get these things, I will become _____."
  ("weak," "a loser," "a worthless nothing")

In this exercise, what I want you to do is let God reveal the lying voices that are keeping you from coming home to him— voices of false gods that may right now be holding your soul in bondage so you are not set free to grow. If you continue to listen to their standards and their agenda, you may never be free enough to return to God, or hear his assessment of you, or experience his healing in your life.

Every man among us needs to return to God our Father, to turn our backs on the so-called "party" and learn to listen only to his voice again. How do we do this?

CLEAN SWEEP

Kyle recognized that he'd been worshiping for many years at the altar of a macho image. A long while ago when his girl-friend, Melina, became pregnant, he was furious, feeling as if she "let" herself get pregnant to trap him into marriage. Melina protested that this was not the case. Kyle loved his Harley, drag racing, and hanging with a tough crowd. No way was he going to give all that up to push a stroller and change poopy diapers. With no career of her own to fall back on, Melina easily gave in to his pressure to have an abortion. A decade later, Kyle still fights those voices that dictate how "a man" acts—to the extent that he even pushes his wife, Jill, away when she wants to hold hands in public. "It makes me feel stupid," he protests, although he knows it crushes her feelings.

Chip can go for a time enjoying the modest home he and Lorraine have built in a comfortable neighborhood—but then the old voices go off inside: *If you spent less time with the family, you could do better. You know you can do a lot better.*

The thing about false gods is that they don't give up easily and they don't go away without a fight. We must remember we've built a pretty substantial relationship with them. Jesus taught his followers to beware of spiritual influences and relationships that pull us away from God. Sure, we can resist them once—but if we're not careful, these forces will return with reinforcements and hit us seven times harder than before. What we need to do, Jesus said, is to make a clean sweep within (see Matthew 12).

Here are some important steps we need to take with God:

Agree with God and His Judgments

In the story of the Prodigal, the son woke up to the fact that his father's plan for him had been right all along. His own plan

took him to the gutter, where he'd been forced to eat slop to
stay alive. Likewise, we need to agree with God that what we've
taken into our souls, trying to fill our empty longings, has been
slop because no image, no success, no escape can fill and satisfy
us within. Nothing but God himself can do that.

We also need to agree with God's judgment that we're
embracing false gods if we let the world define and train us in
what it means to be mature, healthy men. Give your manhood
to the world, and you will be pulled apart. Return to God, and
you will be on the road to becoming a new creation under his
guidance and training.

Agree with God's Assurance of Mercy

After the Prodigal took the courageous step of going home to
his father, he realized that there was mercy and hope for him
in his father's house. Most postabortive men live with dark
whispers that tell them God wants to harm them or people they
love—to pay them back for hard-heartedly taking the life of a
child.

Joe confesses that he lives in constant fear that God will take
his beautiful four-year-old, Elisabeth, from him "to get back
at me for aborting my first child eight years ago." Even though
Joe can say he believes God is merciful, in his heart he hears
another voice telling him not to trust God too much because
God just might give him a sucker punch by taking Elisabeth's
life.

We must recognize and silence any voices that seek to keep us
from trusting God totally and freely. When we return to God,
he does not want to punish us for the sin of abortion—and he
most certainly will not harm or kill those we love in order to
"get" us. Instead of drawing back from him in fear, we need
to return to our place at the Father's side, seeing ourselves as
beloved sons of God.

Yes, it's true that the Prodigal made a wholehearted, no-
holds-barred confession. His father had seen him coming up
the road while he was still a long way off. With heart pounding,
the father ran down the long lane of his estate and threw his

arms around the weak, dirty, stinking straggler—who sank
into his embrace. Looking into his dad's eyes, feeling intense
shame, the young man blurted, "Father, I've sinned against
you and against heaven." He begged his father to take him
back—if only to live in a barn at the back of the property—
and let him feed the livestock.

"Please, Dad. I just need to be near you again. I need to be
home."

Imagine the tears streaming down the face of this broken-
hearted father. "My son has come home," he whispers. "My
son who was dead is now alive again!"

Instead of punishment, the Prodigal Son gets a party. The
real thing this time.

You and I cast ourselves on the mercy of the Father when we
face him and offer our own full-hearted confession. We are
granted God's mercy when we stop blaming, dodging, excusing,
and rationalizing . . . and state the full, ugly, unvarnished
truth: We ran from him because we didn't want to live his way.
We thought we had a better idea. We hated his restraints and
rules. We wanted freedom to get exactly what we wanted out
of life. And if a child got in our way, we took its life . . . or
allowed it to be taken. We then blamed the woman, or bad
timing, or even God himself, for the act we committed. We
alone sinned against others, and against God.

You may be thinking, *But I didn't choose the abortion. I had no say in
what happened.* If you are a man who did not choose the abortion
of your child, you may be carrying resentment, anger, and
blame toward the woman who did. These powerful emotions are
like pellets of plutonium powering our reactions to life from a
deep-core place. Perhaps you have not known why you carry
anger, maybe even judgment, toward "nice guys" or toward
women. Now is the time to ask God to help you forgive and
release the woman who decided to end the life of your child. It's
also time to free yourself from the prison of angry resentment
that has held you. Your bitterness, however "justified," is causing you to limit and sin against your own soul, your own life.

It's time to return to him. Time to accept the Father's

welcome, to hear that he still accepts you as a full son and as
a man. Time to be welcomed to his side.

HOME, WHERE THE HELP IS

With honest, full confession we bring our full selves back
before God at last.

Confession allows us to acknowledge and own up to the evil
we participated in and the ways in which we continue to let evil
influence and direct our lives.

Confession means more than owning up to our sin, because
God quickly gives a merciful response. Once we have acknowl-
edged our wrongdoing, we must also accept that we now need
the empowerment of a merciful heavenly Father in order to
become full sons of God. It's the ongoing, daily empowerment
of his grace—and nothing else—that will keep us growing toward
mature manhood.

Confession leaves us standing eye-to-eye with God. We have
come home to him. We've stopped writing our own misguided
ticket to manhood, and we're ready to agree with him on vital
issues regarding what it means to be a man. We will look at
this—our ongoing spiritual training and the elements of com-
pleted manhood—as we move along in the book.

But for now, we need to look at one final element of the
Prodigal's story—something vital for every postabortive man
to grasp.

The end of the story shows us that the Prodigal Son had a
prodigal father. If you did not know it before now, *prodigal*
means "lavish." We saw that the son was lavish in wasting his
money on the stupid nothings this world offers. But there was
more lavishing to come.

When the son finished his confession, the father called to his
butler, "Run into the house and get my best new suit, the one
you picked up from the tailor yesterday. Then get these rags off
my son, help him shower, and dress him. I want him to look
like a million bucks."

By now the kitchen help had come outside to see what the
commotion was about. Turning to the head cook, the father

said, "I know you bought a huge roast the other day, and you were saving it for the dignitaries we have coming in—but forget it. Tonight we're feasting! Make sure you have all my son's favorite foods on the table."

Then, as the son reeled and the servants scrambled, the father looked at the ring on his own finger. A signet ring, embossed with the family crest—signifying all the ancient honor and dignity of their line. Slipping it off, he pressed it onto his son's ring finger.

"Welcome home, Son," the father said.

Just as this father lavished his son with blessings, so God longs to lavish you with all the blessings of spiritual manhood that he has had in mind for you from the beginning. He wants to clothe you in dignity and honor. He wants to feed your inner man, to fill your need for acceptance, respect, and love. He wants to mark you in the eyes of others as a man of purpose with strong masculine identity and spiritual authority.

Today it's time to come home and dine at your Father's table again—to receive the father's blessing you've always longed for.

QUESTIONS

1. Think back on your own spiritual journey. Have you, in your own way, been like the Prodigal Son? In what ways?
2. What false gods have lured you away from your Father's presence?
3. Why do you think false gods have been so appealing to you?
4. In what ways have false gods let you down or fallen short? What have you learned from your experiences?
5. How has God been good and merciful to you regarding your abortion experience?

Seven

God of Our Deepest Needs

Imagine a scene like this:

One day, Jesus climbed a hillside overlooking the Sea of Galilee. The sky had a touch of haze, signaling a chance of rain later. He'd speak to the crowd that had come to listen this afternoon—your average group of Western tourists and vacationers— and send them on their way before supper.

Jesus scanned the crowd—in particular, this day, focusing on the men. A guy in khaki work pants and a blue shirt looked bored and checked his pager. Three guys in biking clothes were joking together and balancing mountain bikes against a rock. One man in a business suit looked especially frustrated as he talked rapidly into his cell phone.

And as he looked on their faces, he saw into their hearts— hearing every need, every anxious thought, every doubt.

What am I doing here? If Jesus knew the kind of life I've lived he wouldn't want me in his crowd.

I really hope he can't read minds because my fantasies aren't exactly Sunday school material.

Man, I've really blown it with God.

What would Jesus say if he knew I'd agreed to have my own child aborted?

And hearing all this, Jesus still taught them, saying, "Blessed are the poor in spirit—the men who know they are not 'good enough'— for theirs is the kingdom of heaven. . . . "

The wonderful thing about the message Jesus brought is this: God comes to meet us at the point of our deepest need. That's what it means to be "poor in spirit"—empty of our hubris, self-justifications, arrogance, and blame. It doesn't work if we try to meet him in any other way. No one can give us something we won't accept—not even God. And what we need, when our souls have been wounded by abortion, is a whole new approach to living.

If you are a postabortive man and want this new kind of life, you have to let God show you how he alone can meet your deepest needs. You need to acknowledge that, on your own, you tried to meet your needs in the wrong way: by becoming sexually involved before you were ready to be a whole, responsible man in the first place.

THE STEP NO MAN WANTS TO TAKE

To this point we have looked at how we need to turn from false gods and return to the presence of the true God, our Father. Yet, living with God from today on will place more demands on us. It may be some time before the echoes of the old voices die away. In the meantime, we will continue to live with old inner hungers.

Life comes from filling inner needs, as well as physical needs—and from giving to meet the needs of others. For that reason, we'll turn our attention in the next chapter to the ways God, our Father, begins to fill us with a new identity, allowing our souls to feast on the good things he has for us . . . making us into new men who are strong and growing from within.

The next step we need to make with God in our consequential journey is to let him show us how to be vulnerable again.

We need to be gut-level honest with ourselves about our fears and insecurities. The difficulty is that admitting weakness—even to ourselves—is a step most men don't like to take. It's too scary. It goes against our ingrained habit of self-defense and our need to preserve the status quo.

And yet it is one of the most freeing, healing steps toward wholeness that we *can* take. Here are several examples of what I mean:

LEON. Leon admits today, "From junior high on, I always needed to have a girlfriend. I was so insecure about myself, and having a girlfriend made me feel important. It's no wonder I used my high school girlfriend, Sharon, for sex. The way I saw it at the time, that made me a *real* man.

"I didn't feel like much of a man the day I dropped her off for the abortion—and then drove away so no one I knew would see me there.

"The truth is, I'm nearly forty now, and all these years later I still feel insecure a lot. I brag to other guys and make my successes better than they are. I keep measuring my worth by what the world says success is—my income, my house, my car. It took me a long time to admit how much I care what other people think of me. But once I saw that, I realized how much time and energy I've invested and how many stupid things I've done to look good for other people.

"Seeing that about myself was an important step in getting free from it."

WALT. Walt's weakness is that he deeply resents anyone who has authority over him. He fears that they will not have his needs and interests in mind or treat him fairly. As a result, he can't work for anyone but himself. Because when he works for a company, he's always at odds with either "the man in charge" or with the rules and policies.

It was this same weakness—the inability to trust authority—that caused Walt to think he didn't need the morals of the church he was raised in. It also led him to think that sex outside marriage was all right for him and his girlfriend—even though their relationship ended in pain and anger, with an aborted child as a consequence.

Walt says, "I kept bucking authority all my life. In a disagreement I was immediately angry and argumentative—many times even with my business clients. Rather than seeing someone else's point and rather than admitting when the client was right, I had to win every disagreement or at least get the last word in. So I didn't get a lot of repeat business.

"When it came to disagreements, something deep inside would tell me these people were trying to take advantage of me . . . even though my mind would be telling me, *They have a good point. You should give in on this one, Walt.*

"It took a while to recognize my deeper problem: a really deep distrust of anyone in a position over me. A belief that they would use me and hurt me if I gave them a single advantage. Even though I thought I was winning, I had a losing attitude. That was hard to face."

GERRY. Gerry lives with a buried fear that every girlfriend he has will someday leave him. It's much like the fear of abandonment that drove him to have sex with his college girlfriend, believing that it would bond her to him in some permanent way. That relationship ended in an abortion and an ugly breakup.

"Now I keep doing things for my present girlfriend, buying her things. But all the while I think no matter how much I do for her, I could mess up someday, and then she'll meet another guy and walk out on me.

"Underneath it all, I'm scared of being alone."

TONY. Tony's fear of responsibility has driven him most of his life. His playboy attitude led him from one bed to another all through his twenties, with several abortions along the way. But now, past forty, he can't settle into a long-term relationship and face the responsibilities of a family, even though he'd love to have children.

"I'd love to have a son. But I refuse to get trapped into some boring, thankless, dead-end job with other people depending on me to support them. Growing up, I lived with my uncle, and he had to work like a rat on a wheel to make ends meet.

"For me, making that kind of commitment spells death."

ERNESTO. Ernesto was fourteen when his older brother was killed in a gang-style slaying in New York. A year later his best friend died of cancer at just sixteen. "I was just getting into

girls, really. And I hate to say it this way, but I decided I was
going to get as much sex as I could, while I could.

"I kept thinking, *Tomorrow I could be gone just like [my brother and best
friend]. What if I don't get the chance to have a really good time?*

Today, Ernesto and his wife are at odds about the raising of
their sons. Though Ernesto is a strong Christian and teaches
his sons that sex is for marriage, his wife is angry that he's "way
too permissive" in other ways.

"She says I can't say no to my three boys. That I've spoiled
them and they're lazy. It's true, I guess. They're doing poorly
in school, and my oldest can't get into a decent college. They
have a lot more than they need, and they don't even appreciate
it. But I keep thinking, *They're only kids once.* She says I'm not pre-
paring them for real life.

"Lately, I've realized my big mistake. I've been afraid of seeing them unhappy because they can't have something they want.
So I've been Santa Claus when I should have been training
them to work for the things they want. That's how it works in
real life."

Each of these men has a considerable weakness because of an
underlying fear. Fortunately, each is now willing to face the
attitude that first led to the sin of abortion and later caused
continued damage in other areas of life. These men need to let
God show them how to be open and honest about their innermost needs. Only then can they learn to trust him to show the
way to fill their driving needs.

It's only as we *receive* the blessing that overcomes our brokenness—that is, the blessing that comes through a no-nonsense,
direct relationship with our Father in heaven—that we can give
a blessing to the ones we love.

REVISITING

One way to become open to God—that is, open to his welcome
and care—is by asking him to help you revisit your experience
of involvement in the abortion. Before now, you may have
thought back fleetingly to that time, or you may even have vivid

memories of visiting the clinic. On the other hand, you may
have been an unwilling participant or may not have been told
about the abortion until it was over. But I'm talking about
something more than physically revisiting a particular place.

Most of them have never gone back to revisit their involvement in abortion *in order to examine their attitudes and emotions at that
time or to perceive the event as God perceives it.* In a sense, both the abortion and their whole inner state at that time have remained
locked in a sealed room—and they've taken great care to avoid
it. Who wants to open up a room with that much discomfort,
fear, and unpleasantness inside? The thought of it may raise
their anxiety level or make them feel angry.

When God invites prodigals who are "poor in spirit," to
come home to him, he doesn't let postabortive men back in the
door only to shame them for what they've done. His is a true
"welcome home" in every sense. But at the same time, it's crucial that he show the real weakness involved in abortion in the
first place. Relationships include restoration as well as celebra-
tion. Only then can they begin the right kind of inner healing,
taking steps to close the wound that continues to weaken their
lives as men today: Finding their weakness can show them the
direction of healing and new growth.

As you consider revisiting your own experience, it may
encourage you to see how this step helped Jake.

JAKE AND MARYANNE. About to graduate from medical
school, swamped with massive student loans and an intern's
grueling schedule, Jake encouraged his fiancée, MaryAnne, to
abort an "unplanned pregnancy." Having been raised in a very
religious, moral family, MaryAnne did not want to embarrass
herself and her family, and quickly agreed. Afterward, with the
pressures of finishing medical school and then starting into
practice, it was relatively easy for Jake—who tended to be cool
and analytical anyway—to put the event out of his mind.

But an event like abortion does not simply go away.

A couple years after Jake finished medical school, he and
MaryAnne were the parents of a two-year-old son. And their

marriage seemed to have more than its share of disturbances.
Communication was poor. Jake felt MaryAnne had little interest in sex. An air of estrangement hung between them.

Then the dreams became an issue.

For some time, MaryAnne had endured the terror of a
recurring nightmare . . . which grew more vivid and violent
until she woke up in tears. It was always the same:

She was floating in a warm ocean . . . feeling the waves peace-
fully lulling her. . . . Suddenly . . . a dark shadow, circling in
the water . . . a huge body slamming into her . . . the shark's
teeth tearing her apart . . . blood in the water . . .

In time MaryAnne made the connection between the dream
and the abortion and began to seek help. Jake, still the cool
analyst, downplayed it as part of MaryAnne's "more emotional"
nature. But then, keeping a cool, aloof professionalism as a
doctor was something on which he prided himself.

Several more years went by before a chance event triggered
something deep inside Jake.

MaryAnne's close friend was vacationing at a lake when a
sandbank collapsed, pitching her children into the water.
Tragically, her three-year-old son drowned.

When Jake heard the news, it was like a powerful fist had
punched him in the soul. Every day, as a doctor, he'd made
life-and-death decisions and seen many tragedies. Maybe
it was the mental picture of an innocent little boy playing,
unsuspecting, on a sunlit bank above a peaceful blue lake,
then plunging to his death in the chilly waters. It was all so
cold—and it caused something inside Jake to crumple. He
wept and wept.

During med school, while studying the wonders of the human
body, Jake had been convicted that there must be a Creator.
After their marriage, MaryAnne had become more involved
in her church; Jake, though not religious, at least left himself
open to God. Now, for the first time, he began to pray. *Why is
this happening to me? Why am I falling apart over this kid's death?*

One day while driving to the hospital, thinking of nothing
but his morning rounds, he was surprised by an answer that

materialized out of the blue. *You're experiencing pain now, at the death of this little boy, because the baby you aborted was a boy . . . your first son.*

Veering over to the curb, Jake leaned his head against the steering wheel. A pain welled up from deep in his stomach . . . and tears. Alone, he wept for his lost son, saying over and over, "I'm sorry. I'm so sorry."

That was just the beginning of healing for Jake. Seeking a Christian counselor, he was able to revisit the time of the abortion—to prayerfully walk through not only the events but the attitudes and emotions that had motivated his actions. It was the first time Jake had made himself *this* open to God.

It was also the first time he had allowed himself to feel the pain of the event. Deep inside, his spirit had always sensed the terrible tragedy and loss of the child's life—but Jake had blocked the pain to keep himself from feeling it.

Blocking pain is, of course, a very human and self-protective reaction. As we saw in an earlier chapter, men use many things such as alcohol, drugs, and other escapes to "medicate" and numb interior pain. To begin healing, Jake needed to see how his cool and aloof attitude (*I must keep an objective, unfeeling distance from the pain of human struggle, suffering, and loss*) was the self-centered stance that drove him to pay for the death of his first child. Rather than endure the added struggles of having a baby while still going through med school, rather than face the pain of family embarrassment, Jake had let an icy reason coat the decision to abort. His emotional coolness kept him from connecting to the child he'd fathered. Cold objectivity helped him anesthetize the sadness, pain, and guilt that comes when one is responsible for killing a child. Interestingly enough, despite all of Jake's defense mechanisms, his spirit had nonetheless registered the true horror of such an unnatural act.

It's also easy to see how Jake's chosen painkiller—his ability to distance himself from struggle and hurt in order to make clear-headed, professional decisions—contributed to problems in other areas of his life, such as his inability to communicate on an emotional level with MaryAnne or to experience intimacy with her.

A great deal of objectivity is necessary in most professions—especially the medical professions when human lives are at stake and the best, most rational, and calmly executed decisions must be performed as precious seconds tick by. But the same kind of cold objectivity is deadly in a person's emotional life. Jake's growth to whole manhood began when he opened himself to God and allowed God to reach through the wall of objective thinking and unblock the pain.

Recognizing how his "strength" became his great weakness, Jake has been able to enter into a deeper, richer kind of manhood than ever before—experiencing new intimacy with MaryAnne, connecting deeply with his children, and learning how to know God's presence and help in his life.

A DIRECTION FOR US ALL

How many of us are living only half lives because we've kept the pain of living, the pain of being weak human beings, at a safe distance? How far have we run to keep from feeling? And how much growth have we denied ourselves by not working through the pain to a new level of interior strength and maturity? What's true for the body—no pain, no gain—is just as true for the soul.

What Jake experienced—what we all need to experience—is what the Bible refers to as "godly sorrow" for his sins (see 2 Corinthians 7:10). This is not the same as a stagnant kind of sadness that keeps coming back every few months or a depression that weighs us down for years, making life gray and miserable. *Godly sorrow* comes when we allow God to help us get to the core of a matter—to see into our own hearts where our hidden, self-centered, and unhealthy attitudes are the *cause* of sin and the pain that follows. Godly sorrow shoulders responsibility for the wrong attitudes and for the resulting tragedy. This penetration is a painful process because it cuts to the heart of our sinful weaknesses. It cuts to the place where we know that, without playing any more games, we need something or someone beyond ourselves if we are ever going to be released from the dark area of sin in our lives.

And yet, experiencing godly sorrow is a positive, powerful step toward masculine maturity. Why? Because this kind of sorrow—heartfelt remorse that we made the foolish choice to protect ourselves at someone else's great expense—leads to repentance, as the Bible puts it. Repentance is not simply feeling bad about something we've done; it's making the deliberate choice to stop handling life the way we used to and to take a new course.

> **Repentance is not simply feeling bad about something we've done; it's making the deliberate choice to stop handling life the way we used to and to take a new course.**

In Jake's case, it required him to stop using cold reason to protect himself from personal pain, as if he could live above the stuff of life the rest of us mortals have to go through. The "new course" required him to engage at intimate levels with his wife and children, to learn how to openly communicate his thoughts and feelings instead of hiding them or hiding *from* them. Repentance caused him to stop erecting isolating walls of cold rationalism that cut him off from the emotional and spiritual bonds that connect us to each other.

As a reminder, though, one of the first things you'll experience as your heart thaws is *pain*. Far from being a negative experience, it's a sign that God is doing the work of healing in you. God removes your dysfunctional heart of stone and replaces it with a truly human heart of flesh. "Heart surgery" doesn't happen without suffering and a long-term commitment to following the prescription for recovery. But the benefits far outweigh the costs.

REAL HELP . . . NOW

Often we don't know why we made certain choices in our past. We tend to act reflexively—and a lot of times we surprise ourselves. Sometimes the influences exerted on us by the gods we're serving are so subtle we don't even realize that we've acquiesced to the wrong choice. We don't even know the things we're capable of doing until the pressure is on or no one is looking. This is one reason men who were involved with abortion are left with an uneasiness about themselves— whether they actively chose the abortion or it was someone else's choice. Where did this impulse to protect themselves— over and against the life of a helpless baby—come from? How could any man assent to the killing of what would have been his own child? Do we as men even *want* to know what's really going on in that murky place inside us where this impulse sprang from?

When you are ready to take this step and examine your heart with God, I strongly urge you to do it in the presence of a counselor or pastor. I recommend this because (1) it is too easy to rationalize our actions and remain blind to our inner motives and (2) we may get lost in the darkness. The apostle Paul understood the trickiness of these heart matters when he lamented the surprising, discouraging force of sin in his life: "I do not understand what I do. For what I *want* to do I do *not* do, but what I *hate* I do" (Romans 7:15, emphasis added). A wise spiritual counselor can help by pointing out sinful attitudes and patterns that we can't or won't see in ourselves and can turn on the spotlight of grace when we feel like we're being overcome by darkness.

There are other important functions a spiritual counselor can perform, and we'll consider them in greater depth in later chapters. For now it's worth noting that you will benefit by having someone who is able to hear your confession of sin, witness your sorrow, pray for healing and redirection of your inner attitudes, and confirm God's forgiveness. He can also suggest steps that will help you develop a new pattern of thinking and acting to replace your present, weak, unhealthy, and sinful patterns.

This is the real help we need to be transformed—from our old "fugitive" selves into men who are strong within and growing in godly manhood.

Odd, isn't it, that our growth toward strength in spirit begins with admitting our weakness and our needs. I have to

warn you that, even at this point, our human nature—especially
our tendency to cover up and deny weakness—can cause us to
misstep.

For some guys it can be fairly easy to admit mistakes of the
past. In some ways it can even reinforce an ungodly macho
image, which has nothing to do with the character of Christ
God wants to form in us, his spiritual sons.

For instance, a guy can sheepishly shake his head and say,
"Yeah, I *used to* use women sexually to make me feel good about
myself." Or "I was a pretty irresponsible kid at twenty-three;
that's why I let the abortion happen." This can sound like a
true admission of the problem and even like repentance. But
let's be honest: For some of us, admitting weakness and failure
in the past can be a buy-off—a way to avoid confronting ourselves
now. In admitting only to sins of the past, we can maintain a
front that says, "That was then, this is now. I don't really need
to be vulnerable to God or depend on his help, thanks. After
all, I'm better." This is an artful dodge—a way of saying,
"Really, the sin was committed by another guy. And I'm not
him anymore. So you're looking at the wrong guy—*I* didn't
actually do it."

Becoming vulnerable and learning daily dependence on
God mean admitting the weaknesses and sinful attitudes we
hold *today.* We are most in God's presence when we are living,
confessing, and praying in the present. We are called to admit
the things we substitute now in place of an honest relationship
with God. When we do this, we finally own up to sin. We say,
finally, "I am the man—I did it. And until my heart is
changed, I will keep on sinning against others. Lord, change
my heart."

TAKE INVENTORY

What inner needs drive you today—where are you "poor in
spirit"? God wants to fill those inner needs. What substitutes
have you accepted in place of his provision?

Consider the following statements, and see if they describe
you.

"I Need Approval"

Most men balk at this statement immediately. "Need someone else's approval? No way." We like to think of ourselves as strong, independent men who don't really care about other people's opinions of us. But that's usually far from the truth.

A need for approval can drive a man into bed, where he conceives a child out of wedlock. Then it can drive him to abort the child rather than risking the negative, disapproving opinions of others. And it can go on to drive him for the rest of his life.

Many of us have at least one major area of our lives where the core need for approval pokes through the surface. It may be a need for approval when it comes to our success in business. It may be the need to let other guys know that our politics or theology is "correct." It may be the need to work out until you command the attention of women and men with your extraordinary physique. Some guys are dominated by the need for their parents' approval, even well into middle age. The need for approval can show up in the way we feel we must provide an above-average lifestyle for our families.

In themselves, any of these pursuits can be healthy and beneficial to you and to others. But if the primary motivation comes from an insatiable desire to gain approval, the pursuit can become an idolatry and will never meet the need it promises to meet.

A man's core need for approval can be filled only by learning God's purposes for his life, then living out those purposes to the glory and honor of God.

"I Need to Be Loved"

Many of us grew up hearing the words "I love you," but we never experienced real love. This means we were not cherished, nurtured, or admired, which are the actions of love. Even if we grew up in good homes, with well-meaning parents, most of us experienced deficits in one or more of these areas.

As a result, we reached out for something that looked like love but was only infatuation, or maybe only lust: a pretty face, an available body, an understanding heart, immature words of commitment to "true love forever." If we're honest, many of us knew that what we were getting and giving wasn't real love, but we used love's language to manipulate: "Sure, I love you. That's why I want to sleep with you." What we meant was, "I love the way being with you makes my body feel." We were partly right because sex has a way of making us feel nurtured, admired, and cherished—even if the feeling is only temporary. Men are very vulnerable here because they often think having sex is pretty much the same thing as affirming love. ("If you love me, you'll have sex with me.")

The need for love is always with us. It can be met only as we accept God's pure, consistent, and unconditional love. Apart from that, we'll always be operating with a love deficit, like being "maxed out" on a credit card, so we can't buy even one more thing. Like consumers, we'll be takers and not givers in relationships. We can become givers and experience selfless love in greater depth and maturity only as we become vessels of God's love by giving pure, consistent, and unconditional love to someone else. This requires a lifetime of commitment—a commitment to cherish, nurture, and admire others.

Love is a mysterious power: The more you allow to flow through you, the greater you become. And the more you allow to flow through you, the more your need to be loved is filled. It isn't love when the sex act is more desired than the personal and lifelong commitment of a marriage relationship.

"I Need Freedom"

Many men feel the need to be free from the stuff that ties us down—freedom to be creative and to play. This is a legitimate need for adult men, just as it was a legitimate need for us when we were young men or adolescents. Freedom to play restores the spirit. Many men process grief this way.

However, the need to play and experience fun without serious consequences drove some men to make wrong choices early on. They treated sex as mere play, more or less oblivious to the fact that it was like treating a stick of dynamite like a firecracker. Unless men admit that this need for freedom and fun is a legitimate need, they can ignore it and let it misdirect their whole lives.

Some men—especially those who stay overfocused on sex as play—continue to misdirect this need into the use of pornography for recreational fantasizing, or even visiting adult bookstores or pickup bars or call girls while away from home on business. They tend to minimize the consequences—including AIDS and other sexually transmitted diseases. They tell themselves, *It's just for sport.* Or *I'm a man with a strong sex drive, and I need this.* Or *This allows me to experiment with things my wife won't try.*

With God's help, we can turn this misdirected search for freedom and play toward healthy pursuits and, at the same time, become vulnerable with God about another important need. . . .

"I Need Sensual Engagement"
A man may experience pleasure and release as he loses himself in sublime, physical oneness with another body. Physical bliss erases the emotional tensions piled on us by adult life and even stimulates health-promoting hormones throughout the body. When God pronounced human sexuality good, he blessed the act of sex in every sense.

Part of the act of sensual engagement, though, is to open up honest, intimate communication between two partners who can learn, over a lifetime, each other's secret and often changing needs and desires. For men, who are adventurers and explorers, that can bring embarrassment. What if we open up and tell our partners what we're really thinking . . . or ask them for something we want . . . and they're shocked or horrified? What if your desire for affirmation through sex is unfulfilling to your partner?

Too afraid to risk real intimacy—deep honesty about who we are and what we want—many of us settle for "phantom relationships," even with our own wives. We settle for sensuality without the true soul connection. Because of this, some men carry on fantasy sex with fantasy women while making love to their own wives. Or they simply remain emotionally and spiritually disconnected.

A desire for something experimental or unconventional may be related to a legitimate desire to connect emotionally or to deeply abandon ourselves to oneness with our wives. Nevertheless, it may cause further separation if a man tries to act on something new and exotic without communication and consent. Conversely, in conversation with our wives, we may discover that the new physical approach isn't what we truly desire after all—that what we want is actually a deeper form of emotional intimacy. This can come through a "giving" attitude that desires to please the other. Such an attitude is, itself, affirming.

What we need is a relationship that is truly without shame, the way the first man and woman were created to be. As Adam and Eve looked upon each other's nakedness, they came together in intimate, unembarrassed discovery and experimentation (see Genesis 2:25). This kind of intimacy grows as we overcome our fear of shame and embarrassment, share our intimate dreams, and seek to meet our partner's needs. We need a relationship that grows more sensual over time, and this can happen only in the context of a relational commitment—one that transcends the drive for immediate sexual gratification. Then, not only do we experience fulfillment ourselves, but we become men who fulfill our wives as well. It's important to keep in mind that sexual fulfillment is not love but that love (giving without expectation) will indeed enhance the act of sex.

If we open ourselves to God with this real need, he will give us the courage we need to be vulnerable and honest with our wives—and to find fulfillment for the holistic sensuality we hunger for.

THE MEN GOD MEANT US TO BE

In order to grow, we have to become honest about the forces that drive us. As long as we deny them or pretend they affected us in the past but not now, we're likely to keep filling legitimate needs in illegitimate ways.

I use the word *illegitimate* purposely and in its broadest sense for this reason: It's hurtful and destructive to fill my own need in ways that are self-centered—by hurting, using, or discounting others. It's misdirected to fill my needs in ways that keep me from growing as a healthy man and living in connection with others. And in the end, it is pathetic and unfulfilling to accept poor substitutes for connecting soul to soul as well as body to body when God intends for me to become a whole man, fulfilled in the depths of my being.

If you're wondering why we're considering these deeper matters of the soul, I'll tell you: Onetime turnarounds don't usually change us. What we need is to develop healthy new practices that grow into a whole new pattern for living. This requires us to face core issues and requires time, patience, and practice. New ways of thinking, acting, and living don't come overnight—but following God's pattern for healthy growth gives us that deep soul sense that we are becoming what he intended us to be. Strong. Healthy. Not anxious, needy, and secretly grasping for something to fill ourselves alone, but *fulfilled* and *able to fulfill*.

Fortunately, we have a Father in heaven who is patient with us. He has all the time in the world—and all the graceful empowerment we need—to help us grow. For this reason it's important to understand how he has made it possible for us to become "new creatures," as our old ways of thinking and acting are replaced by a healthy new connection with our manhood.

QUESTIONS

1. In the section titled "Take Inventory," what inner needs did you most identify with? In what ways have you embraced substitutes for filling those needs? How do you think God will fill those needs if you let him?
2. Is sex more important to you than building a relationship with your partner? Is sex more important than building a relationship when it comes to fulfilling your manhood?

3. Why is it important to be honest, open, and vulnerable with your wife about sexual matters?
4. What are two or three key points in this chapter that spoke especially to you? Why did they stand out? What do you plan to do in response?

Eight

New Pathways

New brain research shows how we can actually refashion the
brain. When we learn a new language, learn to program a new
computer, or learn to play a musical instrument, we are actually adding new "hardwired" circuits to the brain. On top of
that, studies show that people who keep learning and growing
tend to live longer.

There is good news in this for the fugitive who turns his
life around: It is entirely possible to change and to become
a "new man." As God revives and remakes us from the inside
out, we can experience remarkable benefits. Some of these are
physical: Doctors have discovered that learning to resolve such
emotional patterns as recurring sadness, anxiety, depression,
and stress can strengthen the immune system, the heart, and
the endocrine system. Incredible how God works, isn't it?
The best benefits, though, are spiritual: We can experience
what it means to be men who know how to walk in step with
God's purposes.

CONFRONTING THE INNER BEAST

We've all heard other men say, "But I've always been this way. I'll
never change." Or "You can't teach an old dog new tricks. I'm
too old to change now." Maybe we've made statements like these
ourselves. Yes, it's true that old habits are not easy to change.
But to believe that we're *stuck* acting and reacting the way we
always have is plain wrong. "I can't . . . " is often a mask hiding
an "inner beast" that can keep us from wholeness and growth if
we give in to it.

I refer to the beast because there seems to reside within many of us a force that wants to hold us back. This can take a couple of forms.

Hopelessness

One is an attitude of hopelessness or despair. A hopeless attitude runs counter to faith. It uses the word *impossible.* It makes us feel foolish for believing we can change. In its darker form, *despair,* it tells us that not even God himself can help us—so we might as well give up and give in to a faithless kind of living, following our own instincts for survival and gratifying our desires without grace.

> **As God revives and remakes us from the inside out, we can experience remarkable benefits.**

Cameron remembers, "You wouldn't have recognized my attitude of despair from the surface. I'm pretty much a happy guy. But underneath it all I didn't believe I could be a moral, spiritual leader for my wife and children. It wasn't just that I felt I didn't have the right—I really felt I couldn't do it. I thought I was just too flawed. So why pretend?"

Cameron had to experience for himself the fact that God can inspire us with new convictions that empower us to take leadership in our own lives and the lives of others. "There's a big difference between being a hypocrite—which I refused to be—and being a man who is learning every day to do what's right. The difference is *humility.* I encourage my kids to struggle to do the right thing the same way I have to struggle to do it. I tell them God doesn't ask us to be *perfect*—that's a word that will make you give up in despair! I tell them God just wants us to open ourselves to his help. And when we feel we can't do it, he'll give us strength."

Rebellion

A second force we may need to confront is a hidden, aggressive strain of rebellion. When it comes right down to it, many of us have manipulated the world to get it just the way we want it.

We've trained the people in our lives to leave us alone when we want our space—or to come near and serve us when we need something from them. So it's not that we *can't* change . . . we just *won't*.

"I always knew how to 'play' women for what I wanted," says Nate. "When I began to seek God's help, I knew that had to change. I had to stop using people.

"At first, I really didn't like that. I resisted it like crazy. Why would I want to change if it meant losing my ability to rule my little world? *No way*.

"One day, I guess God opened my eyes to what a selfish manipulator I was. I *hated* seeing that in myself. Actually, I'd hated it all along. I hated that I had to put on a performance to get people to care for me—because I never knew if they were helping me because they loved me, or if they did it just to get me to shut up and leave them alone. So I got what I wanted, but I never knew if anyone even liked me.

"That's when I began to really change inside. I wanted the people around me to be free to say yes or no without pressure. And I wanted to give without my favor being a down payment on the next favor I was going to demand of them.

"That's probably the first time I understood inner freedom— and love. It felt great. I was like a new man."

Within each one of us lurk the forces that would keep us stuck—laziness, fear of giving up the perks we got when we could manipulate our world and the people in it, fear of being vulnerable, and unwillingness to change. Most of us really don't believe it's impossible to change. We just understand instinctively that change will cost us something, and we don't like to pay the cost.

But if we will not change and grow, the only alternative is to stagnate and become empty shells.

SPIRITUAL SHAPE UP
In the last chapter you faced the pain of the past—the inner weaknesses that led you into immature sexual involvement and abortion. The next step you need to make with God is to follow

his pattern of masculine growth, replacing immature and unhealthy habits with habits that will help your masculine spirit mature.

You may look at all the lost time, all the years you've spent as a fugitive, and think, *Why bother now?* I have some encouragement for you: If you begin to follow God's patterns, working out the weaknesses, you will actually experience accelerated growth.

How is that possible?

First, God *wants* to show us how the old patterns are enslaving. Then he moves to set us free from old patterns that enslave us. He wants to free us from hopelessness and despair, and from our old stubborn resistance to maturity. Before we allowed God into the picture, we were on our own. Now we can count on his help. As Jesus promised, "I will ask the Father, and he will give you another Counselor to be with you forever" (John 14:16). Some versions of the Bible translate Jesus' statement this way: "I will send you the *Helper*" (italics added)—to emphasize that God wants to do far more than offer us advice. He wants to help us learn and strengthen us in areas of living where we're weak.

The point is, God's will is that we change and grow, and that is a powerful force to have on our side.

Second, every step we take toward spiritual manhood is a step toward a place that is rightly ours. As the apostle Paul tells us, we were not created to be fugitives or slaves to old patterns; we were created to be God's own sons, heirs of his own nature, actually sharing in his brilliant glory (see Romans 8:15-16 and 2 Peter 1:3-4)!

Think of it: God has already decided that he wants *you* to inherit a whole new nature—a new way of being!

Taking on this new nature will require struggle, because your old way of doing things always dies hard. Running from responsibility works if perpetual fun is what you're after. (It doesn't work so well if what you want is solid, long-term relationships.) Lying works if you want to escape blame or if you like to get what you want out of people at their expense.

(It doesn't work if you want real intimacy, based on trust.) Suffice it to say, our old ways need to be brought into the light of God's presence, and we must begin to trust him instead of ourselves if we want to find the freedom to change.

The result of our struggle, however, will be that a new nature—the nature of God—will be manifest in us, much the way the glory of God shines from him. (We will consider this more in the final chapter.)

The bottom line here is that we need to embrace the struggle—the pain of growth—the way an athlete embraces struggle. Because it's when we stretch to become new men that we begin to see the work of God in us.

We need to embrace the struggle— the pain of growth— the way an athlete embraces struggle. Because it's when we stretch to become new men that we begin to see the work of God in us.

RUNNING AND ESCAPING

Now we begin to cooperate with the work of God in earnest.

We begin by reversing our habit—which has been to run from the pain and embarrassment of our mistakes and bad choices.

The way we've run from the damage caused by abortion provides a good example. We've escaped the pain with alcohol, work, more sexual promiscuity, and even obsessive religious involvements. We've used many escapes to keep from facing the pain our action or inaction has caused.

Many of us have been willing to stop using these escapes, realizing the damage they cause. But most of us have continued to run from pain and struggle in one other way—by shortchanging our relationships.

- We've learned to end difficult conversations with anger, with stony silence, or by acting wounded.

- Sometimes we've used emotional pressure to make others feel bad and give in—or when they won't, we've bailed out on them.
- We've stormed out on women, ended friendships, cut off our neighbors.
- Some of us have quit one job after another, every time conflict arises.
- Whenever something doesn't work out, we blame the others involved—and then seal our emotions off from other people. Inside, we live in lonely caves of hurt, disappointment, or distrust.
- Or, taking a superior position, we categorize or judge other people for their failures and imperfections. We put them in a social category box, lowering our expectation that any good can come from them. We keep them at a distance.

To say the least, when it comes to building healthy adult relationships, any one of these ways of acting is a very poor choice. And if we give in to these attitudes, we'll remain in our old, fugitive state.

So how do we reverse these relational habits?

OWNING UP

One of the most important, powerful changes we can make is this: *We can learn to quickly admit when we have made a mistake or done wrong and face the pain or problem our action has caused.* It's the reverse of abandonment. The quest to be accountable for, and "own" all that we need to own, is a prerequisite for healing to occur.

The same irresponsibility that led Ellis, at age twenty, to insist on abortion when his girlfriend became pregnant stayed with him in another form for many years: He was irresponsible with money.

While his wife struggled to manage the family's finances, Ellis went out and freely spent a lot of cash on sporting gear and at the stock-car races. When his wife tried to talk it out with him, he would complain about how hard he worked.

"Don't I deserve some fun?" he'd insist. If she pressed him, showing him the unpaid bills and the budget she was juggling, he'd retreat into a joking mood. "Lighten up, babe," he'd tell her, laughing. "Have a little fun."

But the bill collectors didn't think Ellis's spending habits were humorous. By his midthirties, money pressures were wrecking his marriage. He began drinking more as an escape from the tension. His wife moved out with their children and filed for a legal separation. Suddenly the party mood was gone from life, and Ellis grew bitter and irritable.

With the help of a counselor, he was able to stop blaming everyone else for his problems. Together, Ellis and his counselor traced the pattern of irresponsibility and escape that ran clearly through his life. The abortion was one major sign of it—and when he was honest, Ellis could see that his escapism had grown worse every year after that.

Finally seeing himself as a self-centered adolescent, Ellis initially wanted to dodge the added pain of embarrassment. After all, his wife was planning to divorce him. Why not just let her file, and go on?

Fortunately, he realized he needed to act quickly. Ellis sought God's help to reverse the mess he'd created. He asked his wife to meet him at a coffee shop, where he took her hand and looked her in the eye. "I've blown it. You worked so hard to keep us in-line financially. You limited your spending and shopped all those yard sales to buy clothes and bikes and toys for the kids. And I worked against you all the while. This entire mess is all my fault. Will you forgive me?"

Ellis was able to reverse the damage by owning up to his irresponsibility. With continued marriage and financial counseling, this couple is putting their life and home back together.

REVERSING NEGATIVE HABITS

There's an important point to emphasize here: Most of us have a false assumption that we can indulge our irresponsible side and, as long as we're careful or discreet, it won't hurt anybody. For instance, many guys believe it's okay to fantasize and feed

their sensual appetite "as long as I don't hurt anyone." They
tell themselves men will be men, that they can't help it.

In reality, when we indulge in anger, lust, self-pity, or any
sinful and weak thought pattern, we cut ourselves off from the
spiritual empowerment that comes from staying connected to
God. For example, if we entertain lustful thoughts with dream
lovers, we disconnect and withdraw in spirit from our real
flesh-and-blood spouse. If we indulge in self-pity, anger, and
blame shifting, we give up the masculine strength needed to
patiently and thoughtfully resolve conflicts.

Why do we overlook the obvious? Fantasy is a poor substitute
for reality. Fantasies allow us to feel big in our minds, while
acting small and weak in reality. If fantasies of any kind are a
problem for you, begin by taking these critical steps:

First, Train Your Mind and Imagination on God

The Bible promises that we will become stable and strong in
spirit when we teach our thoughts to be "stayed on [the Lord]"
(Isaiah 26:3, RSV).

Make Bible reading a regular habit. As you encounter images
of God, take the time to consider them. When it comes to
overcoming temptation, instead of picturing him as an angry
judge disgusted with your failings, imagine God as a welcom-
ing, supportive, strengthening Father who allows you to draw
close to him in your weakness. Scripture depicts him as:

- a Creator who knows our weaknesses (Psalm 103:14);
- a Physician of souls (Mark 2:17);
- a Brother who understands the failings of our flesh
  (Romans 8:29);
- an Intercessor who empowers us to overcome our frailties
  and weaknesses (Hebrew 4:15).

When lustful images come to mind, God wants us to draw
close to him, not run from him or block him out of our
thoughts. He wants us to ask for his help. He is real and present
and holds the power to change us even when we don't have the

will to change ourselves. He is our healer and our brother-companion. Knowing he does not reject us, knowing he accepts us just as we are, empowers us as we begin to reverse sinful behavior patterns.

Second, Train Yourself to Take Every Thought Captive

This idea, from 2 Corinthians 10:5, means training yourself to be diligent about watching your own thought life. Besides standing guard over your fantasies, you also must stay alert to the thought patterns that have allowed you to excuse sin and weakness in the past. Watch carefully for thoughts such as the following:

- I have a right to _____.
- I'm not really hurting anyone else if I _____.
- I've [worked hard, put up with, done without, suffered], and so I deserve _____.
- It's nobody's business if I _____.
- Sure, God has his rules. But I know the only way to handle this, for everyone involved, is to _____.

Jesus showed us how to take every thought captive during his temptation and trial in the wilderness, when Satan tried to influence his thinking away from God (see Matthew 4:1-11). In every case, Satan tried to get Jesus to focus on a self-centered line of thought. And in every case, Jesus overcame temptation by centering his thoughts firmly on the Father and his divine plan.

William Backus, Christian psychologist and author has found tremendous success in his counseling practice with a biblical form of therapy which helps a client repent, turn from lies, and embrace the truth. Backus helps clients identify the lies or "misbeliefs" they have used to excuse sinful and self-defeating behavior. He helps them replace these thought patterns with truths based on God's Word. Backus encourages people to keep a careful watch over what he calls "self-talk."

Self-talk is what we tell ourselves in our thoughts about

people, self, experiences, life in general, God, the future,
the past, the present. It is, specifically, all the words you say
to yourself all of the time. Backus encourages us to refocus
our thoughts by (1) learning to identify the misbeliefs in our
thinking and self-talk, and (2) replacing the [lies] with the
truth.[1]

Like Jesus, we need to internalize eternal truths from the
Bible. God's Word—which Paul refers to as "the sword of the
Spirit" (Ephesians 6:17)—will help us cut through the self-
centered thinking that lies at the core of our inner weaknesses.
When you find yourself thinking . . .

- *I have a right to* _____. God's Word gives you bedrock to stand
  on. Take this thought captive with the truth that "you are
  not your own; you were bought at a price" (1 Corinthians
  6:19-20).
- *I'm not hurting anyone if I* _____. God's Word, through
  David, shows you the truth about who is offended when
  you go against eternal, moral law. "Against you [God, my
  Father], you only, have I sinned and done what is evil in
  your sight" (Psalm 51:4).

Third, Ask the Holy Spirit to Renew Your Inner Man by Helping You Develop a Holy Imagination

On one hand, we can pray the same prayer offered by David
after his moral disaster with Bathsheba. From the depths of his
being, David cried out, "Create in me a clean heart, O God;
and renew a right spirit within me" (Psalm 51:10, KJV).

Such a prayer conveys our desire to be cleansed of lust,
greed, envy, anger, jealousy—all the attitudes that weaken us
and make us susceptible to outward acts of sin. *God always hears
this prayer.* And if we remain quiet in prayer, allowing his Spirit
to search our hearts, he will point out the sick and self-
centered attitudes that crumble our healthy moral resolve.

On the other hand, developing a holy imagination means
allowing God to show us what our temptation is trying to tell
us about our real need. It is not enough to keep ourselves from

sinning. If we fail to fill our soul's *real* need, we are probably only postponing our fall.

Take Clint, for example, who struggled for years with pornographic fantasies—in particular, images of men dominating women. It fed a cavalier attitude about sex that led to an affair and an abortion of the child that was conceived. Shaken by the event, Clint became a Christian and a hard worker in his church—sometimes marching in pro-life events and helping at a pregnancy center. But it did not stop his unbidden fantasies in which he had total power over a woman. Rather than experiencing spiritual freedom or a sense of forgiveness, he lived with inner agony and shame over his continued weakness.

> **If we fail to fill our soul's *real* need, we are probably only postponing our fall.**

A wise counselor shocked him one day: "Why don't you imagine one of those fantasies right now, and we'll see what the Holy Spirit shows us?"

"Are you crazy?" Clint shot back. "I *know* what God will show us—that I'm a sick sinner."

"No," the counselor insisted, "we need to see what he'll show us about the true need of your heart—something you're trying to fill with these empty fantasies that satisfy you only for a few minutes but leave you empty and guilty."

Clint was able to understand that his fantasies were really a kind of "mind candy"—junk food for thought. When he stepped back from the shame long enough to examine them, he realized that they made him feel powerful, in command, and in a twisted sort of way, sure of his place in relation to women.

With the counselor's help he prayed and began to see that his actual feelings in the presence of women were quite the opposite. In real life he actually felt weak and inept, controlled by women's emotions and, often, their superior knowledge. This resulted in his feeling incredibly insecure around real women. Taking total control through fantasy was his weak, sinful, empty way of trying to fill his real need—to feel confident in himself, equal with a female partner, and admired for his personal and masculine strengths.

With that Holy Spirit-inspired insight into his own need, Clint was finally empowered from within to repent and begin working on healthy, godly ways of relating to real women.

The restoration of the soul's ability to imagine healthy, holy realities is crucial to our spiritual well-being. By taking these practical steps with God's help, we will begin taking on a new nature and become the men God intends us to be.

A NEW VISION . . . OF A NEW YOU

Men who walk this path to godly wholeness notice an immediate, dramatic difference.

As "fugitives," we told ourselves that we, alone, know what's best for us. We convinced ourselves that if our needs for security and gratification are to be met, we must meet those needs on our own, in our own way, thank you very much. But in so doing, we experienced the terrible impact of isolation.

But the new man begins to find that he has God on his side— and literally *at his side.* He is now a son of God, a friend of God, and a partner with God. God has become his mentor, his coach. He is being parented as a man among men with skill, love, and wisdom that few earthly fathers can offer.

I can assure you that when you get real and honest and open with God, the struggle will get intense. Yet, like a good workout, struggling with God to push through spiritual barriers and find new strength satisfies something deep in the masculine soul. When you engage with God, you'll experience the sweat, grit, and excitement of knowing real growth from the very core of your being.

As we said at the beginning of this chapter, God's will is for you to grow.

When guys want to get in shape, a lot of them have a target goal in mind. Maybe it's recapturing something of that physique they had back when they worked out during college. Or losing the gut and seeing a flat stomach again when they look down to tie their shoes. Or to run the 10K in under forty-two minutes. As I've said, holy imagination is a powerful tool in our healing.

As you begin to experience God's help and empowering grace, ask him to give you a vision of the new man you can be. Let him implant in your heart a clear vision of the man you are becoming:

- Because you're learning self-control, you are becoming *safe*— that is, you're becoming an emotional foundation for others who no longer need to fear your unpredictable reactions.
- Because you're learning to trust God, you're becoming *trustworthy*.
- Because you're learning to set aside the impulses of self-gratification to achieve a higher goal, you're becoming *self-sacrificing*—able to care for others.
- Because you're learning to be *loyal*, you are able to remain committed to goals and other people. And because commitment is a foundational component in success, you're more likely to be successful at jobs and relationships.
- Because you're learning to look out for the needs of others, you're becoming more committed to being a *provider*—which means you're more likely to build a successful family because your kids will feel they can depend on you to meet their physical, emotional, and relational needs.

STAYING ON TRACK

Obviously, this kind of growth is not easy. If you want to continue developing in spirit, it helps greatly to have a human trainer to keep you on track. I suggest that you locate a spiritual mentor—what is known in some Christian circles as a spiritual director—someone to keep you on a path of healthy growth when everything in you wants to go back on your commitment.

This may be difficult for some among us, especially self-made men or guys who generally like their privacy. For that reason, we'll look closely at the benefits of a spiritual mentor

or director in the next chapter . . . and how to team with the
right man or group to help you continue in your new growth.

QUESTIONS

1. The author talks about an "inner beast"—internal forces such as
   hopelessness and rebellion that hold you back from reversing negative
   habits. What internal forces have played a harmful role in your life?
   Why do you think they've held such power?
2. If you were to remain committed to the way you are right now, what
   would be the price to your spiritual maturity in the future? to your
   wife and children? to your work and relationships?
3. What does the idea of taking every thought captive mean to you?
   What negative or destructive thoughts do you need to begin taking
   captive right away? How will you go about it?
4. Perhaps you've noticed some positive results already as you begin the
   journey to healing and wholeness. What is God doing in your life
   that's of encouragement to you?
5. What positive changes do you believe God has in store for your
   future?

Nine

A Plan for the Long Haul

Sam Gadless has run the New York Marathon.

Big deal, right? The thing is, Sam was *eighty-five* the first time he competed in that 26.2-mile endurance test. And now, at ninety-three, he has competed in his *thirteenth* marathon.

Besides the fact that he was in his eighties when he started running, Sam's story has other amazing pieces to it. As a young man, he escaped from Poland after the Nazi invasion. By the time Sam was thirty-two, chain-smoking and nervous tension had eaten him alive and doctors had to remove three-fourths of his ulcerated stomach. After more years of chronic pain, Sam had his gallbladder removed, too.

At age sixty-four Sam was retired and soured on living. He'd hated his lifelong profession but never had the nerve to switch careers. Now it seemed all he had left to look forward to was life on a very limited income—near the poverty line—and his chronic ill health. At seventy-eight he suffered from high cholesterol, high blood pressure, borderline diabetes, and severe arthritis in both shoulders.

"My doctors told me I was a mess," Sam reports. "They said I had better change the way I live or I would soon die."

Sam is the last guy on earth you'd expect to set out to compete in a marathon. He could have let regret be his legacy and allowed years of neglecting his health to take its natural course. He could have rolled over and died.

What changed Sam's life was this: *He changed his attitude.* Sam became determined to turn his life around. And despite decades of poor health, he began to tell himself, *It's never too late. And no one is hopeless.*

Sam had the faith to believe he could change. And there was something else Sam Gadless believed. You can see it in the plan of action he took.

Sam had to begin by walking very short distances; in fact, he could barely walk several hundred feet from one park bench to another. Not willing to give up, he took stretching classes and received coaching pointers that allowed him to enter racewalks. He started in the handicapped category. Then he joined several racewalking clubs, where he picked up more tips on workouts, aerobics, and competing—along with a lot of friendly encouragement and support.

Soon Sam set a world record for the 5K in the over-eighty category. But rest on his laurels? Not a chance. Next he sought help and began a nine-month training regimen for the New York Marathon. Two months before the race Sam was hit by a car, but he was undeterred. The day of the race—with his son and grandson alongside to encourage him and help him pace himself—Sam finished the marathon in eight hours and twenty-five minutes.

"The inspiration I got from people calling out my name kept me going," he recalls with a broad smile.

Today, as he nears 100, Sam is a living embodiment of a key truth about living: Training for the long haul requires you to strike a balance between tough-minded persistence and patience with yourself as you grow.[1]

YOUR PERSONAL BEST

Like Sam, most of us have something inside that makes us want to become the best we can be. Somewhere in the past we may have despaired of the goal of becoming better men, but now, with God at work changing us in spirit, our goal can become reality.

Bradley discovered a tension here—tension between the reach for a new identity and the pull of old habits—as he began to heal from the consequences of an abortion he had halfheartedly agreed to eight years earlier.

Recently he stopped shifting the entire responsibility to his old girlfriend. "I could have spoken up and maybe saved that child's life," he admits. "But when she asked me if I wanted her to abort it, I was a bozo. I just said, 'Yeah, that's cool. Do you need money?' Man, do I regret that."

Experiencing God's forgiveness and welcome has been an important first step in Bradley's maturity. The truth is, though, the *steps after that* have been quite a challenge. Bradley discovered he had a habit of freezing inside—a habit of *inaction*—whenever a tough decision had to be made. As a result, time and again he turned over the leadership of his life to other people. He seemed powerless to make good career choices or to get ahead financially. And when it came to serious relationship issues, he angered his girlfriends, leaving them to feel they were "holding the bag" while they needed him to act.

> **Somewhere in the past we may have despaired of the goal of becoming better men, but now, with God at work changing us in spirit, our goal can become reality.**

"I can see my big spiritual issue," Bradley admits. "It's fear of making the wrong decision. I don't think I'm some kind of neurotic, looking for the perfect answer or anything. I just don't want to be wrong. Being wrong makes me feel like less—like I'm not worth much as a man.

"But now that I'm praying again, I keep feeling like God's encouraging me to make decisions and allow myself to make mistakes and learn—something I never allowed myself to do before. I feel like God's saying, 'C'mon, Son, life isn't *pass/fail*, the way you've made it.'

"I know I can become a stronger, better man by learning to be decisive, especially in moral issues. But this is a whole new approach to living for me, and it still feels kinda strange."

No wonder Bradley feels uncomfortable—a bit vulnerable

and awkward—as he takes the next steps on the path of masculine maturity: We need to solidify our new identity as men
who face difficulty and challenges instead of run from them.
We need to learn whole new ways of thinking, of talking out
issues, and of taking responsible action

No matter how long we've practiced the habits of fugitive living, we can develop the new habits that go
along with our new identity as sons of God
growing in our heavenly Father's nature.
Doing this takes time, effort, and practice—
much as Sam's quest to complete the New
York Marathon after a lifetime of physical
ailments. Even with God's help, some of the
deep changes we need will not take place
overnight. Even so, I encourage you to stick
with the process and seek the support of a
wise and godly man who can act as God's
on-the-ground coach, mentor, and friend
to you.

We need to solidify our new identity as men who face difficulty and challenges instead of run from them.

At this point, I believe it's important to
tackle an issue that can confuse some
Christian guys. When we came to God or
experienced salvation, some of us were told that we now had
all the spiritual strength to change and grow that we'd ever
need. We've discovered, however, that we need to learn how
to go on and experience the "new life" God promises us. A
major step in this process is to find the inner walls we've set
up—the invisible, interior boundaries that we use to surround
ourselves for security. What are these inner boundaries? How
do they affect us and our relationships?

Most guys are wary by nature. In some ways this is a charac-
teristic of our God-given role as *protector*. If we're in a public
place and a strange man approaches our wife or children,
our guard goes up. When we sense something's not right,
we're ready to jump between danger and the ones we love.
We're ready to get physical if necessary. This is an example
of setting a *healthy boundary*.

BEYOND THE WALLS

Unfortunately, the boundaries we set to keep threat and danger *out* can also keep help from coming *in*. As a result, we may keep our guard up and hold our private pain and weakness inside when we don't have to. For some of us, it takes a long time to open up and really trust someone else with private information about us—our likes and dislikes, our weaknesses and failures. A lot of guys, even Christians, never get there—not even with their wives.

To overprotect ourselves and our secrets is to maintain *unhealthy boundaries* between us and those who are meant to be part of our lives. This is not only unnecessary, but it keeps us from growing in character, because the people in our lives are placed there by God to help us connect with life and to mature into healthy, godly men.

> **The boundaries we set to keep threat and danger *out* can also keep help from coming *in*.**

Take Loren, for example. As he sought healing from past involvement in abortion, he found it difficult to break through the thick walls of silence and secretiveness he had raised to protect himself from feeling embarrassed and ashamed. After all, if other people knew, wouldn't they look down on him? Think of him as a guy who couldn't control his sex drive or keep his life together? Regard him as a "baby killer"?

In Loren's case, his inner boundary involved the issues of *trust* and *fear*. He could not trust God to forgive him; in fact, he believed that if he faced God, he would meet only anger, shame, and punishment. Not surprisingly, Loren believed he'd experience the same thing with people. His wall of secretiveness protected him from the rejection he supposed would come if he was honest with another human being.

Loren had to consciously, purposely reopen himself to the spiritual realm. It involved a deliberate decision to pray and, in his case, read the Bible for the first time. He had to consciously open his mind and heart to God. "It helped me to base myself in God, so to speak. To understand his character and ask him to help me make it my own."

This spiritual awakening began to translate into real changes in his most important relationships. Loren found that experiencing God's love and patience allowed him, in turn, to be more loving and patient with other people. The walls of silence and distrust began to come down. Loren started to become open and vulnerable to the people he wanted to grow close to, especially his wife. Sure, it was a risk. Honesty always is. The risk to Loren was both *being known exactly as he was* and *being misunderstood and rejected*, but refusing to risk would mean staying stuck inside.

Loren and Judy, now his wife, had chosen abortion before they were married. Even though Judy went along more or less willingly, Loren had really pressed for the abortion. As a result, Judy was left with an inner wound similar to Loren's: She could not trust his decisions. Understandably, because the abortion left emotional wreckage in her, Judy wondered if Loren was choosing and acting only in his own best interests or if he took her needs into consideration.

As Loren came to recognize his distrust and how it built a barrier of silence, he knew he had an important choice to make in his relationship with Judy. He'd always faulted her for the emotional distance. Wasn't *she* the reason he retreated into long silences and held himself back from her? Wasn't *her* emotional state to blame for the fact that, after nine years, their marriage was in serious trouble? He could no longer hide behind that faulty reasoning. In fact, he was squandering his God-given, masculine power to contribute to a healthy marriage.

Loren recognized that God had been patient and kind with him. God had sought him out and given him time to trust and open up again. God had not become frustrated and given up on him. How could he, Loren, do the same with Judy?

Now when Judy hesitated to accept his decisions or acted without asking his opinion, Loren took a new path. Rather than allowing frustration and rejection to build a wall between them, he chose to be patient and understanding.

He told her, "Look, I know you haven't been able to rely

on me when it came to making decisions. And maybe I've been heavy-handed sometimes and pushed you to do things you didn't want to do. I'd like to change that. Can we begin to talk stuff out and make decisions together? I promise I won't force you to do anything you don't truly want to do. Before we act on something, we'll talk until we're both comfortable."

Today, Loren says, "Once I got ahold of the fact that I could open up to God and trust him, I really sensed his patience and kindness. That helped me open up to Judy and be patient and guide her through decisions. It was like God was saying to me, 'Hey, you can trust me to be good to you.' And I wanted [Judy] to experience that kind of trustworthiness in me."

In this way, Loren is walking the path of godly change and masculine growth, which has enabled him to win the confidence of his wife.

As we learn to break down the unhealthy walls inside, we can experience the same kind of inner transformation. Fortunately, God will bring these unhealthy boundaries to light, reveal our self-limiting attitudes and behavior, and nurture in our hearts a desire to break down our walls and become his men.

FRESH AIR FOR THE SOUL

When we experience new, healthy ways of living, it's as if a breath of fresh air has blown in to cleanse the stale air we've been breathing. Rather than feeling that events and other people are controlling our feelings and actions, we begin to realize that God is giving us the power of godly self-control, which the Bible refers to as a "fruit" of the Holy Spirit's work in us (see Galatians 5:22-23). This new strength empowers us with the ability to direct our feelings and actions with strong, healthy, mature responses to life. What we're talking about here is working in cooperation with God toward building new character into our personalities.

One great sidelight of these changes is the sense that God is empowering us to respond in new ways to life. Because of that

we begin to live with the assurance that we're free from the
penalty of our sins—that a new strength from within is giving
us the ability to live a "new life in Christ."

Yes, we'll still experience negative human passions and
emotions. We're not angels yet. But now we can experience
the ability to direct these inner forces. This is far better than
being controlled by hidden feelings or suppressing them.
Godly self-control gives us the ability to harness the masculine
energy of our deepest motivations for better, healthier use.

A SPIRITUAL MENTOR

Paul says our new life of spiritual growth is like running a race
(see Galatians 5:7 and Hebrews 12:1). In other words, achieving
spiritual maturity requires training and endurance; no one
achieves it naturally or easily. For this reason, smart men and
women through the ages have sought the help, support, and
supervision of a spiritual mentor—a spiritual coach.

For better or worse, much of modern Christianity seems
to encourage a private, individualistic approach to spiritual
growth. While this may appeal to our highly individualized
Western culture, it also fosters an unhealthy degree of interior
isolation. Too many men walk in and out of church every
Sunday, smiling and saying, "I'm fine, thanks," when they're
really struggling and dying inside.

Our problem is that we have natural blind spots and can
deceive ourselves.

Take Gregg, for example. When he sought postabortion
counseling, he strongly denied that he was experiencing serious
depression—until the spiritual director with whom he was discussing his new faith intervened.

"You tell me you dislike your job but you feel stuck," his
counselor said. "You can't get motivated to start projects
around the house . . . or even to sign up for spring softball,
which you've always loved. You're not sleeping or eating well.
You tell me you freeze up and can't make simple decisions that
used to be routine. And then you insist you're not depressed."
The counselor stared at him. "Man, these are classic symptoms

of chronic depression. Why is it so hard for you to see yourself in this light and ask for help?"

Gregg blinked hard and swallowed. "Because the church I grew up in taught that depression is a sin. Because my dad raised me to believe that men don't give up and give in to emotions—they just shake it off and stay at it. Because . . . , " and here Gregg's resolve finally crumbled, " . . . if I admit I'm depressed, some doctor is gonna push antidepressants on me or tell me I need psychiatric help. I *hate* taking pills . . . and I'm definitely *not* crazy!"

All the mental conditioning Gregg had received growing up, from his church and his father, told him that men don't get depressed—especially Christian men. Stacked on top of that were Gregg's natural dislike for taking medications and his typical male-ego resistance to admitting to a weakness or emotional struggle. In short, Gregg was compelled to see himself as emotionally strong in order to view himself as a man—in particular, as a man of faith in God. All this added up to one huge blind spot that kept him from being truthful about his true condition.

Having the spiritual director, who was an older man and a member of the clergy, gently confront Gregg with the truth was very important. A friend or peer most likely would not have had the same ability to step behind Gregg's defenses. It's also important that Gregg's spiritual mentor was firm with him and not soft. Someone who's soft on us, such as a close friend or peer, may back away from the truth as soon as they sense our discomfort. We need someone who will see what we won't see about ourselves and will gently "blow our cover" by insisting on the truth. You'll also notice, from the manner of Gregg's counselor, that being firm doesn't mean becoming brutal. He didn't label Gregg as good or bad, strong or weak, spiritual or unspiritual, sane or nuts. He didn't try to plow through Gregg's denials. He just mirrored the facts—holding up a mirror of reality so Gregg could get a real good look at himself and discover himself in an atmosphere of safety.

After Gregg's resistance speech, the older clergyman said kindly, "It won't kill you to admit it. And it doesn't make you less of a man or less of a Christian. In fact, I commend you in a way. You've been fighting a hard battle with this depression for a long time, haven't you?"

In short, the man showed Gregg the respect he needed in order to feel safe letting down his guard. Rather than force Gregg to admit his condition, he simply invited honesty.

This was the healthy support Gregg needed in order to admit that the sadness and depression from past abortion issues had been weighing him down—and the encouragement he needed to take new steps toward a more mature honesty about himself.

THE MENTOR AND THE MINISTRIES

Every one of us can benefit from having someone we recognize as a true spiritual authority. For most men, this will most likely be another man. As we face our own postabortion issues head-on, we need someone who understands the ministries of *soul care, reconciliation,* and *absolution* (or forgiveness) for our sins.

Let's examine the mentor's role and these important ministries more closely.

A spiritual mentor is someone who is trained in the art of guiding someone on spiritual paths that lead closer to God. Sometimes a person with this gift and calling may be referred to as a spiritual director.

A spiritual mentor commits to walking with you through the ups and downs of life. He pledges complete confidentiality, making it safe for you to discuss anything and everything—the best and the worst about yourself. He offers unconditional love and acceptance; he will never reject you because your temptations and sins are so bad. Such Christlike acceptance allows you to be genuine and honest, providing a healthy release from past social training in which you felt the need to put on a good front so others wouldn't think badly of you. No matter what secrets you divulge, the spiritual mentor will always be, ultimately, "for" you.

But this unconditional love is only the beginning of the spiritual mentor's role.

Soul Care

In contemporary culture, the term *soul care* is often used to mean discovering what feels good and right to you, and pursuing self-fulfillment—even if that means going against God's moral order and those things called the Ten Commandments.

The goal of the spiritual mentor is just the opposite of the goal professed by today's false gospel of self-fulfillment. Instead of justifying unhealthy or sinful behavior, the spiritual mentor remains alert to the self-deceptions we all practice—the lies we tell ourselves to excuse our mistreatment of other people or our disobedience to God. Sometimes he may confront you about the ways you stress yourself by living a crazy and out-of-balance life—ways such as overspending, overworking, overplaying, overspiritualizing, or oversensualizing.

In addition to helping you see your failure or sin, the spiritual mentor will help you get to the real root of the problem. This usually involves recognizing some wrong belief or lie you're telling yourself about God and/or what's "owed" to you in life or by other people. It takes patience and careful listening on his part to get to these often subtle attitudes that ultimately, have so much power to direct your actions—as we saw in Gregg's case.

After helping you identify the weakness, immaturity, or sin, the spiritual mentor will redirect you in a positive spirit. That means helping you turn away (repent) from the way you've been thinking about life and the way you've been acting, and helping you take on the new attitudes and character qualities God has in store.

Not all people are suitable to be spiritual mentors—even if they happen to be members of the clergy or know the Bible. In an earlier chapter we looked at some general qualities you should look for in the person whose help you seek in healing from the damage of abortion. Here are some more specific qualities I encourage you to look for in a spiritual mentor. Look for someone who is . . .

- not a new Christian, but someone who is well ahead of you
  in spiritual knowledge and at least somewhat ahead of you
  in life experience;
- skilled at listening long and deep, without quickly judging
  or labeling;
- wise enough to see through surface appearances and
  manipulative words in order to identify false beliefs, lies,
  and idols that are empowering your hidden motives;
- morally and spiritually firm enough to call wrong choices
  what they are—sin against God, others, and yourself;
- able to point out how false beliefs and sins are spreading
  to other parts of your life.

The real benefits of this kind of deeply honest, confessional
relationship are powerful. Confession diminishes the power
of sin until it is broken. It demolishes the false idols we live to
serve.

Reconciliation

After guiding you through a truthful encounter with yourself,
the spiritual mentor guides you on the next important step: to
reunite (reconcile) with God, with others you've wronged, and
with the new man you are becoming. This involves leading you
to a deeper surrender to Christ's authority and power and to
a radical change of heart.

A spiritual mentor helps you personalize and internalize the
Word of God. This means consistently speaking the truth to
you about your heart attitudes and life situations, since truth
is the best "medicine" to heal the diseased thoughts that lead
to unhealthy words, actions, and habits. He may also suggest
Scripture readings or regular Bible study.

Like Jesus, the quintessential spiritual mentor, the one you
rely on should constantly point you back to God's Word as you
form new thoughts and attitudes about life.

A spiritual mentor—like a good doctor—also recommends
actions that can help you cement your new attitude in a new
behavior. This may involve things such as

- telling the truth to correct a lie;
- refraining from making a commitment until you can keep it;
- keeping a commitment you've made even when it's hard or inconvenient;
- refraining from anger, woundedness, silence, and other manipulations you've used to keep people at a distance when they touched issues that made you uncomfortable;
- learning to be generous with your time, attention, and money instead of spending these commodities only on yourself;
- finding ways to make peace with an enemy;
- finding ways to become friends with someone who is different or who makes you uncomfortable;
- developing a character congruent with the integrity of the commitment made.

As you can see, the point of these actions is to turn you away from former attitudes and old behavior patterns. For that reason, these actions will *stretch you* and—like pushing through a physical barrier while training for a long-distance race—help you push through old interior boundaries you once set to protect yourself or to get what you wanted.

Jesus was famous for "prescribing" such actions for people. When a rich young man sought Jesus' direction to lead him on the path to God and spiritual maturity, Jesus shocked him: "Go, sell your possessions and give to the poor" (see Matthew 19:16-22). Jesus knew, apparently, that this young man's overattachment to money was killing him spiritually. (Incidentally, there is no record of Jesus giving this direction to anyone else.)

The point of such direction is to help you practice a new pattern of action that will help solidify your new attitudes. A spiritual mentor can help you overcome negativity, despair, and self-pity when the road to change seems long and challenging.

Absolution

A spiritual mentor can also speak the words you need to hear—saying what God would say if he were to speak in an audible voice to your specific need: Pronounce the graceful truth "Your sin is forgiven, and your soul is clean of its stain."

Why is this important? Because it has the effect of freeing us from the load we've carried in our spirits until now. When we don't admit our wrongdoing, we carry anxiety, shame, guilt, fear. When we speak about our guilt, we are finally owning it before God. Even as we agree to take necessary steps to reconcile with God and others, such as those discussed above, it's crucial to know we're forgiven and clean in God's eyes so we can continue to enjoy his welcome and presence every day. The mentor's spoken assurance that God forgives our confessed sin allows us to experience that inner freedom with God.

As you can see, the ministry of the spiritual mentor is important in our journey to spiritual maturity.

GET OUT OF YOUR HEAD

As you seek to grow in Christian manhood, it can be dangerous to stay in your own head and not allow someone else to know your innermost thoughts and motives. The natural tendency of most men is to keep their thoughts very private. But on our own, our pathologies and tendencies toward sin and weakness generally get worse, not better. Left to ourselves, even the most spiritual among us will tend to serve God only in ways that make us comfortable.

Left to ourselves, even the most spiritual among us will tend to serve God only in ways that make us comfortable.

For that reason, I encourage you to make definite steps to act on your new knowledge and convictions. Take it slowly and carefully, and rely on the wise counsel of a spiritual mentor to help you. With help, support, and the right steps, old habits will give way to new. As we've seen, a spiritual mentor can become the coach who helps you train to "go the distance."

QUESTIONS

1. What things are in your life right now that make you think, *I'll feel real regret if I don't change these things?*
2. Have you erected walls inside your heart that have kept you from recognizing God's call to wholeness? What are they? How have they kept you from accepting his help, or the help of a Christian mentor?
3. What are some specific ways in which you think a mature Christian mentor would be of help to you?

Ten

Man the Blesser

As the postabortive man follows the steps we've laid out so far, he finds that two good forces are at work within.

First he finds himself healing from the aftereffects of abortion; then, at a more basic level, he finds himself getting in step with God. Where before he felt fragmented and defective, he now feels a sense of wholeness and with it something he's rarely experienced: a settled contentment about himself and life.

In a very real sense, a man who learns to walk in step with his heavenly Father experiences the power of God's blessing. What is this power? How does it work in our lives?

GOD BLESSED . . .

Many men struggle with questions such as Why am I here? or What's my purpose in life? This can be especially true for postabortive men, who have been running from themselves and their God-given responsibilities for years. Now, as they learn to walk with God, they can make yet another step in their healing journey: *They're ready to step into their roles as sons of God, where they find their most basic purpose for being.*

The book of Genesis tells us that God said, "Let us make man in our image, in our likeness, and let them rule." God then blessed Adam and Eve, saying, "Be fruitful and increase in number; fill the earth and subdue it" (Genesis 1:26, 28).

Most of us understand that God blesses. But many of us have missed the fact that he also made man to be a "blesser." You and I were made by God for the purpose of blessing others.

In ancient history this ability was taken very seriously. We see this in the story of the patriarch Isaac. His blessing was considered so important that his younger son, Jacob, figured a way to ace his brother, Esau, out of Isaac's all-important blessing (see Genesis 27).

You and I were made by God for the purpose of blessing others.

What does it mean to bless?

According to the American Heritage Dictionary (1982), to bless someone means "to give honor and respect." It means "to confer well-being and prosperity." And it can also mean "to set apart for God's purposes."

Strong's Exhaustive Concordance of the Bible tells us that the ancient Hebrew word for *bless* also means "to speak praise for" and "to offer acts that honor someone."[2]

When you boil it down, to bless someone is to act and speak in ways that lift his soul so he experiences a deep-down sense of acceptance and well-being.

OUR POWER TO BLESS

Our past involvement with abortion conveyed anything but this kind of benevolent goodness. Instead, our action or inaction said to our unborn child, "Your life is not as important as my life or the life of your mother." We conveyed to our girlfriend or wife, "I don't want to use my financial prosperity to care for you and our child. Other uses for my money are more important to me than supporting you and a baby." Choosing our own purposes over God's, we brought death and continued harm instead of blessing.

As a result, many of us who have children live with a constant, dull sense of guilt when we are around them. When we want to do something nice for them, we think, *How can I be good to this child, when I let another child die? Am I just a hypocrite to act like a good and loving father now?*

So in this, our next step with God, we turn the picture around. We begin to overcome shame and guilt by using our God-given power to bless.

Man's power to bless is not like the explosive, creative power

that God has. We can't speak quasars and worlds into being.
It's not some magical force by which we alter nature or reality.
Ours is, however, the power to bring forth life. And after we've
brought new life into being, we have the power to bless that new
life. We can

- confer emotional health by giving honor and respect;
- confer physical well-being by providing, protecting, and
  caring; and
- confer spiritual health by giving godly direction.

So it is that when we step into our role as blesser, we begin
to direct all the godly powers at our disposal to bring incredible
benefits to our wives and children—and even to our grand-
children.

The good news is, every postabortive man can become a
blesser. No one is excluded. The unmarried guy who treats
others with respect and dignity confers blessing. The man
who uses godly influence in politics or social service can convey
protection, care, and spiritual direction to the lives of others.
Married men can begin to bless in their own families and, later
in life, help younger fathers learn the ropes.

It comes down to this: Anything we do in the support of life
and health brings blessing.

TAKING A STEP BACK
For a number of postabortive men, stepping into the role of
blesser can mean taking a step back in time. Some of us feel the
strong urge to bring a godly perspective to our past. For both
Josh and Bud, this took an unusual form.

JOSH. For many years after paying for the abortion of his first
child, Josh closed down emotionally and spiritually. It was easy
to hide in the playboy lifestyle of southern California where
he lived, running from painful memories and using drugs and
alcohol to mask the inner emptiness.

Years later he married Sonya, and she became pregnant.

But all was not well with the baby growing in her womb. "There was a problem with the placenta, and I worried about the baby," says Josh. "When our son was born, he was only three pounds, but he was a fighter. I could feel my chest swell with love and pride, but it was also like a horrible pit had opened up inside me."

He'd seen pictures of what an abortion does to an unborn child. Some babies were burned by saline solution, others torn apart by suction or by steel forceps. "As I held my newborn son, I was coming apart inside. He was no different from the baby I'd allowed to be torn apart."

The pain was terrible. "I could see myself as I had been back during the abortion. Six-foot-two, healthy, and I didn't lift a finger to help my own baby. Instead I paid money to have him butchered. I couldn't take it—thinking about what my first child went through while I walked free."

Now Josh had to face questions about his ability to be a good father to his newborn son. Could he ever be free to play ball with this little boy? to play and wrestle? to teach him to fish? Without help, Josh knew, guilt would always make him hold back. How could he escape the sense of certainty that he would always leave a disappointed, downcast look on his son's face?

Struggling with the painful memories, Josh finally opened up to a postabortion counselor. During his weeks of counseling, he began to have a vivid, recurring dream: *A little boy approaching him, holding up his arms, wanting to be held.* In one session the counselor led Josh in an imaginative prayer session, asking Josh to revisit the dream as they prayed together. Josh could describe the child in detail, even the warm smell of his hair.

"Why don't you ask God to tell you the boy's name?" the counselor suggested.

Josh replied in a choked whisper, "I already know his name. It's Joseph."

A dam broke inside Josh that day. The pain of pent-up emotions—the guilt and agony he'd refused to face for years—was finally being released.

Just as important for Josh's growth, giving a name to his unborn child let him experience himself in the role he could have played in that child's life—as a blesser. Before, he'd only been able to see himself irresponsibly sending a nameless, fatherless child into the void. Now, by "owning" his child and naming him and repenting of the grave sin of withholding the blessing, a greater healing came.

That day Josh experienced a deep sorrow. Guided by his counselor, he brought it to Christ in prayer and experienced the kind of inner breakthrough only Jesus, the merciful Savior, can give.

Men need to give blessing just as they need to receive blessing from God. Josh needed to bless his aborted child with a name and with legitimate membership in his lineage. In time, he felt free to be the father he wanted to be—to see his efforts to bless his new son mirrored in the shine of a little boy's face.

BUD. Bud had long carried the feeling that the child he and his wife, Lindsey, had aborted early in their marriage was a little boy. After a period when he didn't go to church, Bud had begun attending again and had experienced some growth toward spiritual maturity. Then the sudden death of a small boy in the neighborhood brought a surprising wave of grief.

As the neighbor's son was laid to rest with a suitable funeral, Bud felt convicted that his own son had been denied the same care, dignity, and respect. He and Lindsey sought the counsel of their pastor, who listened with heartfelt interest. Taking their hands, he surprised them with a highly unusual suggestion. "We must have a dedication service for your baby."

Bud and Lindsey were surprised. In their church's tradition, a dedication service was an act of great significance. "But," the pastor added, "we'll need a name. Why don't you take some time to think about it and let me know."

Only a day later, Bud awoke with a name fresh on his lips. *Michael.* Since Lindsey was still in the process of considering, he decided to wait and not mention it.

A week later he brought up the subject. "I think God gave me a name for our child—"

"Wait," Lindsey interrupted. "Let me show you something." She'd made a habit of writing down unusual dreams in a small journal she kept by their bed. Emerging from the bedroom, open journal in hand, she said, "Just last night I had a dream. A voice was speaking, and all it said was 'Poor Michael. . . .'"

On the day of the dedication, the pastor went through the form for the dedication service for Bud and Lindsey's son . . . Michael. Bud read a letter in which he poured out his heart and soul to his first child. Watching him, Lindsey glowed with a joy and peace she hadn't experienced in years. For the first time, Bud had brought the blessing of God to someone's life.

"The pastor told me he believed there was great rejoicing in heaven that day," says Bud. "I know I felt cleansed and free inside. And I knew I would see my son again someday."

These stories may have a controversial edge for some readers. The concept of going back in time so someone can experience a "healing of memories" has had strong opposition from some quarters of Christendom. And the idea of holding a dedication service for a deceased child, or learning the child's sex via a dream, or receiving a name supernaturally, may not fit your theology. But the aborted child was not nameless to God, and giving the child a name may help to cement in the parent's mind the fact that the aborted child was a real person and so help the grieving process. By retelling these stories, I'm not advocating the practices. And I'm certainly not encouraging you to mimic what these people have done. But I am asking you to bring your guilt, your grief, and your sorrow to the feet of Jesus. He will show you how the promised forgiveness and healing will become real in your life.

We grow in spiritual maturity as men when we learn to have a profound respect for all life. Josh and Bud, and others like them, took an important step toward healing when they "paid respect" to their aborted children in the presence of Christ.

BECOMING A BLESSER

There is one other meaning of the term *to bless*. It is "to bring glory to." In the most down-to-earth terms, that simply means having the ability to bring a shine to someone's face. As husbands, fathers, and grown sons, there is something intrinsic in our masculine nature that loves to bring a smile, a glow of happiness and delight, to someone's face. We see this at work on many levels.

C. J. delights Ben, the boy he sees through the Big Brother program, by surprising him with something Ben has wanted for a long time: a new baseball glove. He turns to see Ben's mom smiling with gratitude and contentment. And C. J. experiences a sense that he's "done well" for this little boy.

Burt has knelt with his children at their bedside every night since they were toddlers, patiently passing on his faith in God and his belief in the truths of the Bible. When his eighteen-year-old son comes home to say his girlfriend ditched him right before the senior prom, Burt is crestfallen for his son—until the boy says, with a wry smile of victory, "No, Dad, it's a good thing. She was pressuring me to sleep with her. You always taught me right and wrong, and I know God doesn't want that. I actually feel pretty good about the whole thing right now."

When the happiness, strength, or moral direction we pass on to another brings a light to the face, happiness to the heart, or godly courage to the life, we have brought great blessing. Married or unmarried, every man has the ability to bring a godly blessing to those in his world.

For many of us, though, using our ability to bless others doesn't come naturally. Then how can we take this step?

First, Make the Choice to Bless God

God is the source of all our deepest joys. The happiness we get from this world—say, from a new bass boat, a big raise, or season tickets to our favorite NBA team—will not last long. Only focusing the energy of our soul on God, making it a regular habit to worship him, will tap into the kind of joy that lasts forever.

King David wrote, "I will bless the Lord at all times; his

praise shall continually be in my mouth" (Psalm 34:1, RSV). But blessing the Lord begins by honestly searching our innermost attitudes, where a lot of God-dishonoring thoughts can lie hidden.

Rick had to admit that he secretly believed God gave him a raw deal by giving him an angry drunk for a father. For most of his life Rick blamed his father's abuse for the irresponsible attitude that had caused Rick to choose abortion. Ultimately, he blamed God. He used to say, "Hey, my old man didn't love me, and I didn't want a kid till I was ready to love him. If God hadn't made such a messed-up world, stuff like this wouldn't happen."

When Rick turned to God and took responsibility for his actions, his attitude changed. Today he says, "Even though the upbringing was bad, God still gave me *life*. And I believe he brought good people into my life to help me get free from the mistakes of my past. Once I began to serve God, the stuff I did wrong in the past—I was pretty violent and bad to people—actually made me want to help other people more. Only God could do that in my heart. Only he could bring good out of all the wrong I did."

We bring God a lot of happiness when we stop lying to ourselves and excusing our actions and reorient our lives around the truth (see 3 John 4). And we literally bless, or glorify, God by focusing on the truth about his goodness. That invariably leads to blessing others in our own world.

Second, Make the Choice to Bless Other People

As we grow in the knowledge that God has been good to us, we're more likely to become generous with that goodness and more willing to pass it on. That's not to say that it comes easily, even though it's a step men recognize as important in their spiritual growth.

Grady still feels kind of awkward encouraging the guys in the music store where he works. A lot of the other guys are on head trips, hacking on each other all the time. Grady's the standout, telling the other clerks when they're doing a good job and paying attention when they talk about their personal problems. At a surprise birthday party for him, three of the guys stood up to say how much his encouragement had given them a boost to get through rough times. Once a depressed introvert, Grady now seems to embody the blessing of moral support and encouragement.

Now that Evan has resolved his old anger at God, he's developed an ability that even his upper managers are beginning to notice: He has a knack for calming down the angry loudmouths at work by listening to and affirming them. He deftly challenges them to put their angry energy to good use by finding a solution to their problem. This brings peace to the office and better direction to guys whose anger might otherwise tank their careers.

Ron is helping a friend who has made big mistakes in his marriage. Helping the guy face what he's done wrong and standing with him as he makes amends are helping to restore the blessing of love to a troubled marriage.

Third, Make the Choice to Learn Self-Control

All this talk about becoming a blesser and bringing peace and encouragement sounds great, doesn't it? Learning to draw our sense of blessing from God and becoming generous and good to others is important. But learning to be a blesser also involves learning when it's wise to *say and do nothing* as opposed to giving in to old forces within and doing something destructive. Here are some ways in which learning self-control can make you a blesser:

- *Learn to master your anger or other emotions that cause you to lash out.* When someone puts you down personally or attacks someone you love, learn not to retaliate or give in to rage. Instead, practice giving the patient answer.
- *Learn to master fear, self-pity, depression, and other emotions that cause you to withdraw from godly support.* Instead, practice being honest with others when you need emotional support so you don't give in to old, fugitive behavior patterns.

- *Learn to master lust.* The attitudes we pick up in the media toward women very often reinforce that unhealthy side of us that can see women as objects for our use. Take an honest inventory of the books, magazines, videos, Internet sites, and relationships that provoke lust in your heart. Then seek the support of your spiritual mentor or accountability group to help you make ruthless changes where necessary.
- *Learn to master your ability to make and keep commitments.* Yes, there will always be times when a temporary conflict prevents you from having a "perfect attendance" record. But learn how to study a commitment, gauging the real time and energy needed, *before* you make it. And learn how to sacrifice for the benefit of others *after* you make the commitment, even if it means leading the Bible study when only two out of twelve guys show up or sticking with the youth group when it seems no one's listening and you want to quit.

As you make these efforts, I can assure you that you will experience the help and presence of God as he matures you in these parts of your life. Paul reminded his young friend Timothy that God has given us a spirit of self-discipline (2 Timothy 1:7).

Finally, Make the Choice to Be a Caregiver
Many of us have entered adulthood with an independent and self-centered attitude. We've said, "I can take care of myself, thanks. I don't need your help." And we've carried a corollary attitude, even toward people we're close to. Without our ever saying it, our lack of caring and our disinterest communicate what we really think: *Don't look at me. Take care of your own problems.*

William adopted this attitude right after his college girl-friend coldly announced she was aborting the baby they'd conceived. Inwardly he told himself, *Nobody in this world really cares about anyone else. Why should I care?*

After that, he went through several relationships with women. One after another walked out on him in tearful frustration, saying, "I've never met a more uncaring guy in my life." His response was always a bland "Whatever."

In William's postabortion counseling, he realized that if he was going to bless the people in his life, he needed to make a conscious choice to become a caregiver. But even after he checked his callous attitude, changing old habits still involved a big effort on his part.

Most of us men exhibit a more garden-variety lack of caring. We just don't take the time to notice, or we assume no one needs our help or support. Or, really, we hope they'll just leave us alone. Here are some simple things you can do to cultivate the heart and habits of a caregiver:

> **One of the greatest steps to maturity a man can take is to step into the role of blesser.**

- *Take time to notice the needs of others.* Letting someone know that you're aware when they're hurt, sad, struggling, or in some other need is the most basic form of caring.
- *You don't need to take over, but you can offer help.* Taking over someone else's responsibility is not the answer. Instead, offer the blessing of counsel, help, support, advice, and a helping hand and strong back when necessary.
- *Whenever possible, empower someone by showing him what he's capable of doing on his own.* We empower by giving constructive help—not criticism, judgment, or superficial flattery. Empowering is what teachers, coaches, trainers, and mentors do when they talk us through steps while offering both praise and constructive criticism.
- *Above all, be there and be loving.* To say you care and then be absent during a time of need doesn't square. Or to be there with the attitude of a boss, judge, or critic—well, you might as well *not* be there. The caregiver who is strong in presence and love truly blesses the people in his life.

One of the greatest steps to maturity a man can take is to step into the role of blesser. To do so is to regain the position we ran from in our immaturity. It is to "father" in others many of life's essentials—skills, healthy attitudes and self-images, a sense of acceptance and support, and the security of knowing someone else truly cares.

Seeing where God can take us is exciting. You and I can work alongside him as sons in step with our Father to bring blessing into the lives of those we love. In so doing, we will experience an ever growing sense of well-being as the damage of abortion is overcome in us.

QUESTIONS

1. Read Genesis 1:28-31. What did Adam and Eve have to do to be blessed by God?
2. How do you think blessing your lost child can help bring healing to you?
3. When was the last time someone blessed you? Describe what that person did and how it made you feel.
4. Who in your life comes to mind as someone who needs a blessing? What can you do today or tomorrow to be a blesser?

Eleven
The Vision before Us

The magazine cover pictures a slick-looking guy in a fantastic three-piece suit. The confident smile, great clothes, expensive watch—everything about this guy says *success*. You've got to admire him.

The designers who create these covers know they have about one second to grab the attention of a newsstand browser and to fire their message deep into his subconscious mind: *If you buy our magazine, you can be as successful as this guy—in business, in bed, in life—and enjoy the admiration of others.*

People who create these images know one important thing about the human psyche: An image can make a powerful impression and motivate you to do almost anything the image makers ask. However, whether you make yourself as successful as the guy on the cover is completely up to you; the only change they are interested in is that you change your money into their money.

We are motivated by strong images because they speak to needs and desires deep inside us. When we began this book we saw how abortion turned us into fugitives running away from the journey to healthy manhood. Now we're learning to face the consequences of our choices, actions, and inactions. Step-by-step we're opening up to the damage we've allowed, to our pain and loss, and to deeper levels of honesty than we've ever known. We're also learning how to stand face-to-face with God and accept his godly direction as it comes to us personally and through others such as spiritual mentors.

As we close this book, I want to encourage you to keep moving on your personal journey to masculine maturity. What we've been talking about is not a slick, superficial appearance but a powerful inner transformation. And so I want to plant in your mind a vision of the path ahead and the type of man you can become as you continue to grow inside. Because *inside* is where the only significant growth takes place.

THE TWO-STROKE ENGINE

As we are remade from within, our masculine growth will always have two important parts to it. If we miss either part, we'll be like the two-stroke engine that lacks power, misfires, and stalls out.

The first part of our growth is the transformation we're experiencing today. By reading this book or working with a counselor or spiritual mentor, you might be experiencing some pretty heady and dramatic growth right now. Whenever you make an important step—say, learning self-mastery as we discussed in the previous chapter—the change within can feel huge, as if you've catapulted into maturity all in one step.

COLE. For instance, Cole had come a long way since receiving counsel for postabortion issues. He had recognized the escape patterns he used, especially when financial responsibilities seemed overwhelming. Talking it out with his counselor and with an older spiritual mentor enabled him to recognize the moment when inner discomfort over money turned into a desire to drink or spend money he didn't have. It had been this discomfort—a fear of "not being able to provide"—that had triggered the panic in him years before when he pressed Cindy into getting the abortion. Now, working on the weakness and his sinful patterns, Cole could see big changes.

Instead of feeling like an out-of-control adolescent, he now felt a solid sense of masculine identity. He could manage money shortages like a responsible adult and not give in to immaturity. Instead of raging or blaming or partying, he was able to pray and draw on God's acceptance to help him gain self-control. He could make calls to creditors and calmly talk out payment plans when necessary. If one of them was rude or belittling, he didn't give in to self-pity. Cole held on to the fact that he was a true son of God now, working to make amends in his life no matter how long it took and whether anybody besides God believed in him.

Cole was indeed experiencing a big growth curve in his life, just as many of us are. If you are taking steps to face yourself and your past sins and weaknesses, you have a lot of courage. Many people like to hide their sins and keep running from themselves their whole lives. They live on excuses. Scratch the surface just a little and they'll tell you how life and God and every woman they've ever met have done them wrong. But taking the path to spiritual manhood takes guts and faith and humility because it means exposing the things inside that are definitely not easy or pretty. And standing before God, honest and ready to follow godly direction, takes a great deal of strength when everything in this world tells you to take the easy way out. If, like Cole, you've begun to grow in spiritual manhood, you are to be commended.

> **If you are taking steps to face yourself and your past sins and weaknesses, you have a lot of courage.**

Yet there is a second aspect of our healing that you must know about in order to maintain a right vision of where you're going from here: Our healing and growth are ongoing; in fact, they will continue throughout our entire lives. We are new men in God, deepening and growing every day.

This fact about our growth should give us hope and keep us alert for chances to stretch and deepen.

SONNY. Six years ago Sonny experienced major changes with the help of a Christian counselor. As a teenager he'd gotten a girl pregnant. He had told her not to do anything rash, that he would think up a plan before they told their parents. But then panic paralyzed him for weeks while his girlfriend pressed, "What are we going to *do?*" Then came the call from a pay phone one morning: She had taken matters into

her own hands and aborted their child. For years Sonny ran
from the pain of his baby's death by using recreational drugs.
Depression and a brush with the law eventually drove him to
seek help—and his life seemed to turn around quickly. He felt
close to God again and began a new life.

But on a recent trip to the zoo with his wife and two-year-
old daughter, Sonny had an unhappy surprise. As they ate
lunch at a picnic table, they saw a little boy playing tag with his
father—a child whose features and coloring were so much like
Sonny's that even his wife remarked, "That boy could be your
son." In fact, the boy was about the age Sonny's first child
would have been if not for the abortion.

That innocent remark, and seeing this child, touched off
things inside Sonny that he could never have expected. A rush
of pain and helplessness came back—that vulnerable confusion
that had wiped him out after the abortion. For the rest of the
afternoon Sonny fought feelings of failure, guilt, and shame,
all the while pretending to have a good time with his wife and
little girl. What had happened to the profound healing he had
experienced? to the sense of God's forgiveness? to his growth
in maturity?

Fortunately, Sonny had learned how to handle setbacks.

First, his counselor had emphasized that echoes of pain and
remorse are inevitable in the healing process. Something—or
nothing at all—can trigger a memory flashback, flooding us with
all the images of the past. Along with the old images can come
the old feelings, slamming us with nearly the same force they
did back then.

Echoes of pain and remorse are inevitable in the healing process.

In response to old memories and old
feelings, Sonny had learned to take his eyes
off the past and refocus on the new man he
was becoming. He told himself, *The past is
gone. It can't be changed. I can change only today . . .
and tomorrow . . . by the grace and strength of God.*
This is a good lesson for us all.

Second, Sonny had come to understand
as a Christian that God could redeem even

the abortion experience—and that, in a real and intense way, he was being allowed to experience something of the suffering for sin that Jesus Christ experienced on the cross. When Sonny was a boy, all the talk about Jesus' suffering had never meant very much to him; it was only later, as sin shot pain into his own soul, that he understood what suffering for sin was all about.

In response to pain that recurs in Sonny's life today, he has learned to give his suffering to Christ. To do so, he prays this prayer:

> *"Jesus, I give this pain to you. I can't bear it alone. I know that you are the only One who can bear the pain of the whole world's sins. And I thank you that you took all sin and suffering to the cross with you.*
>
> *"I ask that you will help me carry the pain I feel inside right now. I ask you to redeem the pain that sin has caused. Help me to draw inner strength from you. Make me more compassionate for the pain of others. Make me more patient with my wife and daughter and other people in my life when they sin and fail.*
>
> *"Keep my heart open to you. And change me today into the man you want me to be. Amen."*

We need to learn what Sonny has learned: Our greatest personal strength comes from walking closely with Christ in our weakness and joining our suffering to his. We need to recognize that the pain Jesus felt because of sin is the very pain we feel—and it is this pain that leads us on the path of healing and growth.

If Sonny had not known how to handle the onslaught that hit him at the zoo that day, he would have been left in pain, confusion, and discouragement. He might have landed right back in the pit of chronic depression that had plagued him for years.

HEALING IS BY GOD'S TIMING

It's important to have a right understanding of healing so we can know what to expect as we make progress in the weeks and months ahead.

> **Our greatest personal strength comes from walking closely with Christ in our weakness and joining our suffering to his.**

For most of us, the word *healing* implies a finished act. A small cut heals and leaves no lasting effects—maybe not even a scar. We heal from the broken finger we got playing softball and rarely think about it again. It's a once-and-for-all experience.

But when we talk of healing from a soul-wounding act like abortion, it's more accurate to speak of *regaining health*, or *learning to live in spiritually healthy ways*. What does this mean? The following analogy can help explain.

Your body has a healing mechanism known as the immune system. If it's working correctly, you'll heal from almost any kind of injury or illness at a reasonable pace. Colds will come and go. The strawberry you got on your arm when the ladder slid off your shoulder will fade and disappear in just a few days.

But if your immune system is worn down—say, by prolonged worry, poor nutrition, lack of rest, an aggressive virus, or the onslaught of too many stressors at once—the system fails under the overload. Your body is run down and can't easily heal itself. In fact, the medical community now recognizes that immune suppression may be the underlying cause of many modern-day ailments.

However, if the immune system is boosted, it can be restored to normal functioning. Then the ailments that took over are likely to come under control or disappear fairly quickly.

In a sense, when we follow steps to spiritual healing like those laid out in this book, we are strengthening our masculine souls. We are opening ourselves to God so that he begins to restore the image he created in us: man the protector, provider, and caregiver. When we escape from our self-centeredness and begin, for instance, to think of and care for others, that old prison of self-protection we used to live in seems to be demolished.

One who has experienced the restoration of his body's

immune system can experience rapid healing of major symptoms. But if he wears himself down, or if too many outer stressors attack, the immune system is breached and the individual begins to suffer again. But now there is a big difference: *He knows the steps to take to restore his immune function and how to bring relief from the old symptoms.*

As men who are being restored in the aftermath of abortion, our vision of ourselves needs to include this understanding: We are now men who know the way to spiritual healing and maturity. And in our constant seeking of Christ, we will experience healing and growth. We know we aren't perfect but we take comfort in knowing we are definitely "in process." And when the past and old behavior patterns try to haunt us, we know the right steps to take to stay on the healthy track.

SEE YOURSELF AS A MAN OF ENDURANCE

What I've just described about the body and its immunity is, in a way, similar to what goes on in the spiritual part of our being.

What we men seem to *want* is to experience relief from our symptoms. Maybe it's that we like instant gratification. Maybe we just like things simple and done with because we don't like the ongoing messiness of real life. If we expect instant, once-and-for-all healing—an experience to sling us ahead of everyone else in maturity—we'll be sadly disappointed.

What we *need* is to understand how to live—how to build a lifestyle that fosters continuous spiritual growth and wholeness. Only this will keep us on the path of spiritual health so that our souls stay strong and recover quickly from the blows life delivers. This is how Sonny bounced back from the beating his old guilt and shame delivered that day with his family at the zoo. Developing a *lifestyle* of inner health is far more important than the quick-fix, instant deliverance we'd love to have.

Our real need is to rely on God to give us endurance. In our fugitive days we had no clue that enduring discomfort was the secret to anything, much less to personal development.

We couldn't take it when a good, healthy sense of guilt tried
to drive us to God for freedom and forgiveness. Rather than
endure it, we found ways to soothe away its impulses.

Developing a lifestyle of inner health is far more important than the quick-fix, instant deliverance we'd love to have. Our real need is to rely on God to give us endurance.

Spiritual men have always known that
learning to endure afflictions of the soul—
even recurring waves of guilt—could
help drive them closer to God and to other
people instead of causing them to give up.
The Bible is full of people who learned to
endure the pains of remorse long after the
sinful act was over and forgiven. Each time
guilt came to accuse, they endured its fiery
arrows and became even stronger by clinging
more tightly to the grace of God.

The apostle Paul experienced piercing
remorse because, before his conversion, he
had imprisoned and tormented Christians.
He had even participated in the stoning
death of Stephen, the church's first martyr
(see Acts 7:58–8:1). For these crimes
against God and men, Paul later suffered
great torment. Some have even surmised
that this is the "thorn in the flesh" Paul
refers to, expressing gratitude for it because this pain causes
him to rely solely on God's strength to get him through.

But Paul also knew that if he endured his remorse and let
it drive him back to God, he would not give in to condemning
voices. Instead he would remind himself of the love, forgiveness, and utter faithfulness of God.

Paul also understood that one of the secrets of a strong "spiritual immune system" is to allow God to show us a redeeming
purpose for our sins and failures. Paul saw the grief he carried
for his past transformed when he understood that God was calling him to suffer along with the persecuted church. Risking
everything to bring the hope and compassion of Christ to tormented Christians, Paul became the comfort of thousands of
suffering souls. He even defined part of the healing process as

"forgetting what is behind and straining toward what is ahead" (Philippians 3:13).

In our new view of ourselves, we need to include this understanding: We are men under God's care and direction. If we trust him and follow his guidance, he can bring a redemptive purpose out of our losses and failures.

The greatest healings we will ever experience are not like the miracles you sometimes hear about, such as the guy who's instantly healed from stage-three brain cancer. Our miracles will come as we learn to walk with God in the path of healing he lays at our feet—one day, one step at a time.

SEE YOURSELF AS A MAN IN HEALTHY RELATIONSHIPS

As our spiritual healing depends on learning mature endurance, it also depends on staying in a right relationship to God and other people. This means several things:

- *Resting under God's authority.* Before we returned the care and direction of our lives back to God, we were on our own, living by our wits and calling the shots. Governing our own lives, we made some decent choices and some poor ones. But now, opening ourselves to God's direction lets us experience deep peace as we trust in him to care about our welfare on life's pathways.

This includes learning to trust that God is ultimately sovereign over everyone who is over us—whether it is a boss, a spouse, a difficult customer, or some other person who has a significant influence in some aspect of our lives. We no longer need to wrangle inside when they make a bad call that affects us, or hack them up behind their backs. Instead, we can learn from their mistakes, grow in some aspect of our character, and respond in a mature fashion to bring the best out of a less-than-ideal circumstance.

As sons of God we can develop the perspective Jesus expressed regarding authority. We can respond with the same confidence and peace he displayed when the Roman tyrant Pilate arrogantly

declared his authority to grant Jesus life or death. Jesus said,
"You would have no power over me if it were not given to you
from above" (John 19:11).

- *Seeking forgiveness and strength from God.* Whether from shame
  or hard-heartedness, we once found it difficult to admit
  when we were wrong. Pride blinded us to our greatest
  weaknesses and set us up to fail again and again. Pride caused
  us to blame God and everyone else when the flaw was in us.

As prodigal sons who have returned to our Father, we can
never forget the welcome we received the moment we turned
our hearts back to God. Every day now we need to seek strength
for moral courage—that ability to be gut-level honest with
God about our sins—and willingness to make amends where
we can.

Remembering God's forgiveness of us and practicing it with
others will keep us close to the One who is the strength of our
souls.

- *Living by faith—not by feelings.* When we're down or feeling guilty,
  we're tempted to believe that God has left us. *This is not true.*
  Jesus told his followers: "My Father . . . [and I] will come
  to [you] and make our home with [you]" (John 14:23) and
  "I am with you always" (Matthew 28:20).

Our emotions are not the measure of our relationship with
God. As we continue to grow, we need to remember that our
faith stands on what God has promised: He will never leave or
forsake us (see also Hebrews 13:5).

- *Valuing the things God values.* While the voice of the world tells
  us to love things and use people, God tells us to use things
  and love people. Work, hobbies, home projects, money,
  and possessions—any of these things can get in the way of
  worshiping God or loving the people in our lives. And when
  we do, our thinking and our actions become disordered.

God values people first. When we look for the good we can do, the blessing we can bring to the life of another, we will remain on the track of spiritual maturity.

- *Building bonds of trust and intimacy.* In the past, some of us placed way too much trust in fallible humans and were burned when they failed us. This drove us to bitterness and withdrawal.

Now we're bonded to God by trusting in his overarching care and goodness. Seeing ourselves under his authority allows us to rest more easily in our relationships with others—bosses, wives, friends, pastors—knowing that even if they fail us, we won't be destroyed because we're under God's care. We don't need to run from the imperfection of human relationships. Instead we can grow stronger by staying in relationships and working out the nitty-gritty messes of life.

Chet's experience is a good illustration. Chet had never felt good about himself around his wife, Claire, because he saw her as a good person, while he felt unworthy. But as he healed from postabortion effects, Chet was able to trust God more deeply than at any prior time in his life. This trust in God helped him stop hiding his weaknesses from his wife. Now he learned how to ask for her advice when he was confused and for her prayers when he was hurting.

In addition, Chet had never felt right about confronting Claire with her failures. She was a wonderful and giving person, but sometimes she could be harsh and judgmental about people who failed in her estimation. Inside, Chet had let this tendency build into bitterness and distance toward her. But then his own healing made him strong enough to confront Claire in love with the ways she unknowingly hurt and rejected people. When he finally brought this to her attention, she expressed some anger and resistance, but in the end Chet helped Claire see how this harsh side hurt their relationship.

Learning to trust Claire with his inner thoughts was a big step

for Chet. And it was one he never regretted. For the first time
in their marriage he felt he had both a lover *and* a best friend.

- *Making a healthy contribution to life.* In the past, many of us felt
  sidelined, as if we had no business giving anyone moral
  guidance or advice. Now, as we find purpose, godly
  direction, and order, we know that we have something to
  offer—godly wisdom and human insight gained by tough
  experience. We are not outcasts anymore. And we have
  creativity, intelligence, humor, and that all-important
  measure of grace and understanding that we can now share
  with others who walk a similar path.

Because we have been forgiven and accepted by God, we have
something the world needs: hope and a future (see Jeremiah
29:11). Our growth in maturity will continue as we give to others
what God has given us.

Giving to others what God has given us—this completes the
cycle of growth by working out the reality of what we believe
in our lives. As James reminds us, faith *without works to back it up*
is useless and dead. Giving of ourselves to help others proves
what we believe (see James 2:14-26). When we humbly find
our place in the network of relationships, we take part in
God's redemptive, creative impact on the world and our own
generation. Finding our place in God's work cements our
growth in maturity.

SEE YOURSELF AS A SON OF THE LIVING GOD

The apostle John looked at the men of his generation and
said with amazement, "How great is the love the Father has
lavished on us, that we should be called children of God!
And that is what we are!" (1 John 3:1).

Throughout this book we've taken a long look at rebuilding
our relationship with God in the aftermath of abortion.
When all is said and done, perhaps the single most important
and personally sustaining part of our new vision of ourselves
is this:

We who were once fugitives are now true sons of the living God. We have a home—a safe place. We have a Father in heaven. And every part of our lives is under his care, correction, and direction because we belong to him!

If we dare to think we're now perfect and no longer in need of daily dependence on God, we're likely to either slide back into old ways or become self-righteous religionists. But if we abide in the One who calls himself our Father, he will give us the creative power and balance we need to keep going and growing.

This is the greatest knowledge any man can live by. Let it be the light that guides you on all the pathways of your life.

> **We who were once fugitives are now true sons of the living God. We have a home— a safe place.**

QUESTIONS

1. What relationship has changed most for you as a result of working through the steps in this book? In what ways?
2. List some of the character changes you have noticed, or that others have noticed about you, as you've taken steps on this healing journey.
3. One of the attributes of maturity is living by faith and not by feelings. Can you think of a recent challenge in which God empowered you to set aside feelings and trust him? What specific steps will you take next time you feel overwhelmed by negative feelings?
4. You are a son of the living God. What does this mean to you in everyday life—especially in your healing journey from the aftereffects of abortion?

PRAYER OF COMMITMENT

Dear Father in heaven:
I realize that your kindness and willingness to forgive me go way beyond what I can expect or what I think I deserve. My heart is broken by what I have done, and I want to give my life to you.

Today, I'm grateful for your promise that you will not turn me away, because I am truly sorry for my sins.

Father, I have sinned against you, against my own child, and against my child's mother. And when I live apart from you and your grace, I fail again and again to live as a true son of God—which is the identity you have created for me. When I live apart from you, I fail to bless others, and sometimes cause harm to the people in my life. I'm truly sorry, and I agree with your judgment against the sins I've committed. I'm thankful for the way you have made me uncomfortable, even for the pain and regret I feel. I know this is a sign of your Spirit working in my heart, causing me to long for healing, growth, and change.

I seek your forgiveness now, and I ask you to begin to change me at the core of my being. I ask that you restore the broken image of my identity as a man, as a (potential) husband, and as a father. I seek the blessing that you alone can give me. Please strengthen my will to keep choosing you, to keep choosing the way you want me to live. Help me when there are setbacks. Give me courage when I feel like falling back into old patterns.

I thank you for hearing my prayer, Father. Thank you that you will strengthen and help me. It's in Jesus' name I pray. *Amen.*

NOTES

Chapter Three

1. John Gottman, "The Dissolution of the American Family," as quoted in *Family: The First Imperative*, William J. O'Neill Jr., ed. (Cleveland: The William J. and Dorothy K. O'Neill Foundation, 1995).

2. "Mother-Headed Families: An International Perspective and the Case of Australia," Social Policy Report 6. Washington, D.C.: U.S. Government Printing Office, 1996.

3. Sara McLanahan and Gary Sandfeur, *Second Chances: Men, Women, and Children a Decade after Divorce* (New York: Ticknor and Fields, 1989).

4. "Facing the Challenges of Fragmented Families," *The Philanthropy Roundtable*, vol, 9, no. 1 (1995).

5. "Father Figures," *Today's Father*, vol, 4, no. 1; Gallup Poll 1996, National Center for Fathering, 1996.

Chapter Four

1. Ruaridh Pringle, "Struck by Lightning," *Reader's Digest* (March 1998):150.

Chapter Eight

1. William Backus and Marie Chapian, *Telling Yourself the Truth* (Minneapolis, Minn.: Bethany, 1980).

Chapter Nine

1. Sam Gadless, "Runner's High," *Natural Health* (May 1999): 62.

2. James Strong, *Strong's Exhaustive Concordance of the Bible* (Nashville: Abingdon Press, 1890).

Where to Get Help

CareNet	109 Carpenter Drive Sterling, VA 20164 phone (800) 395-HELP www.care-net.org
Fathers and Brothers Ministries	350 Broadway, Suite 40 Boulder, CO 80303 phone (303) 494-3282
Focus on the Family	8605 Explorer Drive Colorado Springs, CO 80920 phone (719) 531-3400 www.fotf.org
New Dawn Post-Abortion Bible Study	1600 Coulter, Suite 203 Amarillo, TX 79106 phone (800) 354-2240
Josh McDowell Ministries	P.O. Box 1000 Dallas, TX 75221 phone (214) 907-1000
Promise Keepers	P.O. Box 18376 Boulder, CO 80308 phone (303) 421-2800 www.promisekeepers.org
National Memorial for the Unborn	6232 Vance Road Chattanooga, TN 37421 phone (423) 892-0803
Loving and Caring	1905 Olde Homestead Drive Lancaster, PA 17601 phone (717) 293-3230 www.lovingandcaring.org

Loving and Caring is a top source of very helpful material for both men and women who are dealing with the aftereffects of abortion and also other pregnancy- and family-related matters.

ABOUT THE AUTHORS

Guy Condon was a graduate of Gordon College and Wheaton College graduate school. He served as president of Americans United for Life from 1982 until 1991, when he became president of CareNet, a pro-life organization with more than eight hundred affiliate members. Shortly after completing work on the manuscript for this book, Guy was killed in an auto accident. His wife, Linnie, and four daughters live in Virginia.

David Hazard is the founder of The New Nature Institute, which produces seminars and books dedicated to the practices of Christian spirituality and their role in human health and wellness. He is the author of the Healthy Body, Healthy Soul series and has produced several other acclaimed series, including Rekindling the Inner Fire, LifeSkills for Men (Bethany), and Spiritual Formation (NavPress). Among his award-winning titles are *Blood Brothers, A Place behind the World*, and *No Compromise: The Life of Keith Green* (co-written Melody Green).

A graduate of Syracuse University School of Journalism, David lives in northern Virginia with his wife, MaryLynne, and their three children, Aaron, Joel, and Sarah Beth.